Praise for *Inside the Minds*

"Unlike any other publisher – actual authors that are on the front-lines of what is happening in industry." – Paul A. Sellers, Executive Director, National Sales, Fleet and Remarketing, Hyundai Motor America

"What C-Level executives read to keep their edge and make pivotal business decisions. Timeless classics for indispensable knowledge." – Richard Costello, Manager-Corporate Marketing Communication, General Electric

"Want to know what the real leaders are thinking about now? It's in here." – Carl Ledbetter, SVP & CTO, Novell, Inc.

"Aspatore has tapped into a gold mine of knowledge and expertise ignored by other publishing houses." – Jack Barsky, Managing Director, Information Technology & Chief Information Officer, ConEdison *Solutions*

"Priceless wisdom from experts at applying technology in support of business objectives." – Frank Campagnoni, CTO, GE Global Exchange Services

"Aspatore publishes the answers to every business person's questions." – Al Cotton, Director, Nypro Corporate Image, Nypro Inc

"Everything good books should be - honest, informative, inspiring, and incredibly well-written." – Patti D. Hill, President, BlabberMouth PR

"Answers questions that others don't even begin to ask." – Bart Stuck, Managing Director, Signal Lake LLC

"Unique insights into the way the experts think and the lessons they've learned from experience." – MT Rainey, Co-CEO, Young & Rubicam/Rainey Kelly Campbell Roalfe

"Must have information for business executives." – Alex Wilmerding, Principal, Boston Capital Ventures

"Reading about real-world strategies from real working people beats the typical business book hands down." – Andrew Ceccon, Chief Marketing Officer, OnlineBenefits, Inc.

"Books of this publisher are syntheses of actual experiences of real-life, hands-on, front-line leaders--no academic or theoretical nonsense here. Comprehensive, tightly organized, yet nonetheless motivational!" – Lac V. Tran, Sr. Vice President, CIO and Associate Dean Rush University Medical Center

"Aspatore is unlike other publishers...books feature cutting-edge information provided by top executives working on the front-line of an industry." – Debra Reisenthel, President and CEO, Novasys Medical, Inc

www.Aspatore.com

Aspatore Books, a Thomson business, is the largest and most exclusive publisher of C-level executives (CEO, CFO, CTO, CMO, partner) from the world's most respected companies and law firms. Aspatore annually publishes a select group of C-level executives from the Global 1,000, top 250 law firms (partners and chairs), and other leading companies of all sizes. C-Level Business Intelligence™, as conceptualized and developed by Aspatore Books, provides professionals of all levels with proven business intelligence from industry insiders—direct and unfiltered insight from those who know it best— as opposed to third-party accounts offered by unknown authors and analysts. Aspatore Books is committed to publishing an innovative line of business and legal books, those which lay forth principles and offer insights that, when employed, can have a direct financial impact on the reader's business objectives, whatever they may be. In essence, Aspatore publishes critical tools—need-to-read as opposed to nice-to-read books—for all business professionals.

Inside the Minds

The critically acclaimed *Inside the Minds* series provides readers of all levels with proven business intelligence from C-level executives (CEO, CFO, CTO, CMO, partner) from the world's most respected companies. Each chapter is comparable to a white paper or essay and is a future-oriented look at where an industry/profession/topic is heading and the most important issues for future success. Each author has been carefully chosen through an exhaustive selection process by the *Inside the Minds* editorial board to write a chapter for this book. *Inside the Minds* was conceived in order to give readers actual insights into the leading minds of business executives worldwide. Because so few books or other publications are actually written by executives in industry, *Inside the Minds* presents an unprecedented look at various industries and professions never before available.

Leadership Strategies for Executive Search Firms

Leading Professionals on Identifying the Perfect Client/Candidate Match, Overcoming Recruiting Challenges, and Establishing Benchmarks for Success

ASPATORE
BOOKS

BOOK & ARTICLE IDEA SUBMISSIONS

If you are a C-Level executive, senior lawyer, or venture capitalist interested in submitting a book or article idea to the Aspatore editorial board for review, please email TLR.Aspatore.Authors@thomson.com. Aspatore is especially looking for highly specific ideas that would have a direct financial impact on behalf of a reader. Completed publications can range from 2 to 2,000 pages. Include your book/article idea, biography, and any additional pertinent information.

ISBN 978-0-314-97963-6
Library of Congress Control Number: 2007943373

For corrections, updates, comments or any other inquiries please email TLR.AspatoreEditorial@thomson.com.

First Printing, 2007
10 9 8 7 6 5 4 3 2 1

Leadership Strategies for Executive Search Firms

Leading Professionals on Identifying the Perfect Client/Candidate Match, Overcoming Recruiting Challenges, and Establishing Benchmarks for Success

CONTENTS

Building a Next-Level Search Firm

Jeff Kaye

Chief Executive Officer

Kaye Bassman International Corp.

Next Level Recruiting Training

Simply stated, the executive recruiting industry consists of organizations that conduct search work on behalf of an employer who pays a fee for that service. It is our responsibility to find and recruit individuals who are, in most cases, currently working for the client's competition. Indeed, contrary to popular opinion, 99 percent of the people who are placed by an executive search firm are gainfully employed and are not actively looking for a job, as opposed to those candidates who actively seek employment through Internet job boards, newspaper ads, and applicant fee-paid staffing services.

Search firm recruiting levels can be divided into several sections—entry or junior level; functional practitioner; mid-level manager; upper manager; and senior executive. If you are recruiting for a position with a salary of up to $70,000, you are probably looking for a functional player; as you go from $80,000 to $150,000 you are recruiting for mid-management; $150,000 to $300,000 is typical compensation for upper management while salaries above that level are typically for senior management—the level of a true executive search.

The Art of the Search

Clients expect expertise in the art of search. In order for a recruiter to identify the top talent in a given industry, he or she has to be good at research. The research process entails first identifying every company who could possibly employ a potential target. Then, every potential target must be identified. This process utilizes various databases, networking, and superior name gathering skills. Some firms choose to outsource this area because of the difficulty in doing this work. There are only three reasons why a search will be unsuccessful at the fault of the recruiter. The first is that the recruiter does not know who to call. The second is that the sufficient number of calls is not made. The third is that they do not possess sufficient skills to recruit the potential target candidates. If the first area, the research, is not done effectively, then the second or third reasons become irrelevant. More simply put, if you want to catch a tuna, you don't go fishing in fresh water lakes! After a recruiter has identified potential talent, he or she must then evaluate that talent to determine whether or not they fit the technical criteria for the client's job. In addition to their quantifiable qualifications, it is also important to evaluate the client's soft skills—i.e., the subjective factors that determine whether or not they are going to be able to integrate effectively into the culture of the client's organization.

A skilled recruiter must also possess what I call "attraction skills." Once you find a promising candidate, you need to be able to share the kind of information about the client's opportunity that is most likely to woo the candidate away from their present job. Once you have accomplished that feat, you need to be able to navigate the candidate and the client through the entire process of interviewing; making an offer; acceptance of the client's position; and assisting in the candidate's resignation from their present job, which may involve overcoming a counteroffer. Finally, an executive recruiter needs to ensure that the transition phase goes smoothly—that the client is satisfied with the candidate, and that the candidate is happy in their new environment.

For many years, search firms and practitioners tried to differentiate themselves on the basis of their level of expertise and skills as a search professional; however, I believe that every recruiter should be skilled in all of these areas—identifying talent, assessing talent, attracting talent, and handling the interviewing and transition process. If you do not know how to handle these areas, this is the equivalent of recruiting malpractice.

Targeted Recruiting

In my opinion, a superior recruiter is one who has the ability to be an active participant in their client's industry, and is a master of that client's market. Therefore, your market must be small enough that you are able to maintain a level of dominance in terms of industry expertise in that segment; however, it must also be large enough that it can provide you with enough space to accomplish what a recruiter wants and needs to accomplish. For example, if a recruiter says that they have a lot of experience in the health care field, that is a very broad area—he or she cannot possibly be an expert in the entire realm of health care recruiting. Rather, a skilled recruiter will focus on a specific area of health care, such as recruiting for hospitals or pharmaceutical companies.

Within our organization, for example, we have a team that recruits only for hospitals, and each individual within that team recruits for very specific functional areas within hospitals—i.e., accounting and finance; Information Technology (IT); nursing, radiology, pharmacy, hospital management, etc. Each individual will also have control over a specific geographic area, within that function, and within that industry. Indeed, our recruiting process can best be described by the acronym FILL—function, industry, location, and level—and each of our recruiters has to have the right combination of those four criteria in order to ensure that they truly understand their client's market.

For example, one individual in our organization will handle health care finance recruiting in the southwest or southeast, and every search that they work on will be for a CFO, controller, revenue cycle management, or back-office individual. The candidates that this recruiter will look for are not just accounting and finance people that can work for an airline just as easily as a hospital; they are skilled health care finance people whose skill set is specifically focused on finance and accounting for hospitals.

If there are fewer than 500 hospitals in our recruiter's target area, it will not take long for that recruiter to get to know every CFO, controller, and finance department at those hospitals—what their reputation is like; how those hospitals run their offices and their individual departments; and what the culture is like in each department. As a result, not only can that recruiter quickly identify candidates who work in similar environments to that of our client company, they can also identify the individuals that are going to be best suited for that environment—as opposed to another recruiter who many work on only two hospital financial searches in a given year, as well as two for the drug industry, two for the medical device industry, two for the diagnostic industry, and two for the hospital equipment industry. You cannot have the same level of expertise throughout all of those industries. Some recruiters may claim to specialize in hospitals only, but then work across many different functional areas. However, this breadth can make it very difficult to develop an appropriate level of market mastery.

Therefore, what differentiates our firm from 95 percent of all other search firms is the level of in-depth experience and specialization of our search practitioners. For example, some of our recruiters focus solely on recruiting pharmaceutical R&D scientists in one specific area—i.e., one recruiter may focus on formulation science, while another handles only drug metabolism and drug safety searches, and we utilize that granular approach in all of our other searches in a number of industries—construction and real estate, insurance and financial services, banking, call centers, legal, energy, consumer products, retail or any of the twenty plus specialty practice teams that we have in our organization. Each industry has a specific team of recruiters, and each recruiter in each team has extensive expertise within a specific search area. One team even only specializes in placing people transitioning out of the armed forces and into the civilian work force.

Configuring the Search Team

When recruiting for a specific industry, you need to configure the search team in such a way as to be able to accomplish a high level of market mastery. The commercial construction industry, for example, is defined by retail and office strip centers, office buildings, and malls. In that space, it would not make sense to specialize by type of position—i.e., one recruiter for project managers, another for business development, and another for finance and accounting. In this case, it makes more sense to focus on geographic recruiting because positions can blend from one company to another and experience in a specific geographic area is usually critical—i.e., one recruiter for commercial construction in the southeast, another team for the west, and another for the Midwest—and each recruiting area is not so large that our recruiters will be unable to get to know everybody in the field, nor are they too small to be too narrowly focused and niched.

In insurance recruiting, on the other hand, it does not make sense to have a geographic concentration; rather, your concentration would be by function—underwriting; actuarial claims; or sales—and different teams would be assembled consisting of recruiters who have a specialization within those various insurance industry functions. Some industries, however, require both types of recruiting team configurations. For example, one area in our firm of recruiting expertise is health care; one recruiter handles searches only in the northeast and only for hospital pharmacists in that geography.

Indeed, the search industry is just beginning to catch on to what other industries have known for decades—people want to hire specialists. Patients no longer see an orthopedic surgeon; they go to a surgeon that specializes in specific areas such as the spine or the shoulder. Beer companies hire specialty reps that deal with specific distributors such as big box stores, restaurants, or convenience stores. The drug industry does not just have one pharmaceutical sales rep that details all products; it has a rep that details cardiovascular products, and another that handles oncology products.

Recruiters must therefore become experts in their space, as companies increasingly rely on search firms to be experts not only in the generalized world of search, but in the world of search in a specific industry, a specific geography, and at a specific level of candidate.

Assessing Candidates

Before an executive search can get underway, the recruiting team must establish the quantifiable qualifications for the client's position. In most cases, the client needs to find a candidate who has proven that they are effectively capable of doing their job, unless they are hiring for an entry level position, or they are willing to take a gamble and hire someone from outside of the industry—in which case they generally will not need to enlist the services of a search firm.

Let us say, for example, that a bank has an opening in their real estate commercial lending department and they are looking to hire a commercial lender with a good reputation. In such a case, we would try to pinpoint the top ten to twenty banks in their area with big commercial lending departments, and we would then identify the four or five top lenders at each of those organizations—people who are quantifiably doing exactly what the client wants done at their company in that they are all lenders working in the real estate space, and they all have a portfolio sizable enough to meet the client's criteria.

Now let us say that only ten of those lenders are interested in considering the possibility of change. We then have to decide which of those candidates is best fit for the job (the short list)—and what really separates one recruiter from another is the recruiter's ability to uncover those characteristics that make one candidate the best match for their client company. In order to do this successfully, you must really understand the client's culture. Everyone says that they want to hire workers who are team-oriented, driven, passionate, articulate, bright, intelligent, committed, and innovative, but those buzzwords mean different things to different companies. For example, in one company, "hard working" may be defined by someone who is the first person to get to work at 7 a.m. and the last one to leave at 6 p.m. In a second environment, however, that person might be fired for being lazy, because "hard working" in that environment means working fourteen hours a day, rather than eleven. Simply put, there is no one universal definition of "hard working," and you have to figure out what that term means for the specific client company and candidate you are dealing with. Your ability as a recruiter is measured by how well you interpret what the candidate means when they say they are hard working and willing to do what it takes to get the job done; and by your ability to get the client to define what "hard working" means for their department and their company.

Finally, you have to assess whether there is a good "chemistry" and "cultural fit" between the client and candidate. All fits are situational; to say that there are good or bad candidates or good or bad companies is an overly simplistic view of the recruiting process, in my opinion. Lee Iacocca was fired from Ford for being ineffective, yet he was able to turn Chrysler Motors around; therefore, it was not that he was a bad executive—he was just not the right person for Ford's culture and environment. However, he was heralded for his incredible leadership at Chrysler. Some even called for him considering the U.S. presidency because of it. What makes a candidate good or bad is relative to what the client wants; therefore, you have to be able to evaluate both the candidate's soft skills—what we call qualitative characteristics—as well the quantifiable work skills that helps to establish whether the candidate can do exactly what the client wants done.

Recruiting Challenges: Recruiting "Happy" Candidates

Clients typically want to hire people who are successfully working for the competition; however, what they often fail to recognize is how difficult it is to persuade someone to leave a job where they are happy and well compensated. Indeed, the number one challenge of executive recruiting is the fact that the best candidates are not looking for a job—they are usually very well entrenched at their current position. If relocation is also involved in recruiting for the client's job, that makes the process even more difficult.

The only way to overcome this challenge is to effectively utilize your recruiting skills, as well as your knowledge about your client, to get a candidate to at least consider the possibility that making a career change with respect to the client's position has very little downside and a strong upside—i.e., perhaps the client's organization can provide a long-term opportunity for the candidate that cannot be found within their current situation.

Even the greatest recruiter is going to hear "no" multiple times during the search process; therefore, they need to find ways to persuade candidates to consider the possibility that the client's position is an ideal fit for their needs. If a recruiter recognizes that the client's job is not a good fit for a particular candidate, and then starts to engage in unethical sales practices such as failing to disclose information that might jeopardize the candidate's interest, that is not acceptable. However, if a recruiter really knows their market and the client's corporate environment, and they truly believe that the candidate would be much better off personally, professionally, spiritually, and financially by taking the client's job, then they have a responsibility to attempt to persuade the candidate to consider interviewing for the client's job. Some search practitioners simply like to refer to themselves as consultants, but in this case a good search consultant must never forget that it is the search consultant's responsibility to advise, encourage, and persuade—otherwise known as selling!

Compensation Challenges

The second major challenge that recruiters often face is dealing with compensation issues. For example, if the client is offering the candidate a $180,000 salary because that is what they pay other executives at their company, but the candidate is asking for at least $200,000, the client may risk creating internal inequity if they were to agree to the candidate's salary demand. If the other executives find out that they are being paid less than someone who has not been with the company as long as they have, they are likely to be upset.

Indeed, many people believe that if you do not change jobs every few years you will never be as highly compensated as you should be; and they may believe that loyalty does not pay because if you can get a major raise whenever you change jobs, you will wind up making more money at your new job than whatever compensation you may have received after an annual review. Therefore, it can be a major challenge to bring in new people from the outside without compromising the goodwill of the executives on the inside. Some companies try creating a more meritocracy based culture for it is okay to have big differences in compensation, but only based on differences in measurable contribution to the organization.

Dealing with Counteroffers

A third major challenge in the recruiting industry is dealing with counteroffers. In this war for talent, companies do not want to lose good people; therefore, if a candidate resigns in order to work for their employer's competitor, their present employer is likely to make a generous counteroffer, their reasoning being that the employee will not only hurt their company but enhance a competitor. Additional costs would be also incurred if the candidate's present employer has to refill their position—i.e., a search fee that may be $30,000 or even $300,000, sign-on bonuses, equity, relocation, etc.—and they may have to wait many months before the new employee is up to speed.

If a company may face costs of $50,000 to $500,000+ due to the loss of one of their executives to a competitor, it may be much cheaper for them to offer the candidate a raise and/or promotion as an incentive to stay. Although it is never a good idea to accept such a counteroffer, it can be very tempting for candidates to fall prey to such financial wooing. Educating the candidate thoroughly in all of the perils in considering such temptation is critical. Why must they threaten to quit to get the raise? Is this simply a bribe to buy more time to make them expendable? Is their loyalty compromised? These are the types of questions a talented search professional will discuss with the candidate.

Profit Generating Strategies through Retention

If an executive search firm gains expert knowledge in the market that it serves, its clients will be satisfied with the work that it does, and as a result, they will give the agency more work over the years to come, which will help it to build a strong reputation in the industry. I call it the snowball effect:

the better the quality of the work that you do, the more work that you get. Simply put, your "inbox will always be full" if you do your job well.

Indeed, if a search firm achieves market mastery as well as search mastery that gives it an industry-wide reputation, and if it is able to establish long-term strategic partnerships with its clients, then it is more likely to achieve substantial revenues—and as your revenues grow, your profits will grow. Therefore, achieving long-term success and profits in this industry is typically based on ensuring that your recruiters are serving their clients' long-term and short-term interests by filling their positions with quality candidates in a timely manner.

However, even if a search firm does a good job of serving its clients, if it does a bad job with respect to retaining its recruiters, it will fail. Unfortunately, many search firms have high turnover; but if a firm hopes to really grow their revenues it has to retain its recruiters—and those recruiters must retain their clients. The snowball effect applies in this scenario as well: if you are able to retain a number of good recruiters, you will be able to create a better working environment—and you will be more likely to attract quality recruiters to join your company. Any recruiter who is contemplating which firm to join is more likely to join a firm where there is heavy retention of happy recruiters, as opposed to joining a search firm where the average tenure is a very short time relative to the firm's age. In essence, I believe that the most critical element of growing revenues and profits is hiring and retaining top recruiters for your own organization—doing for yourself what you claim to do so well for your clients.

Gaining Market Share

The best way to attract market share away from the competition in this industry is through speed and quality of service. When a client is considering which search firm to use, they will always consider which firm has the ability to expedite their search and enhance the quality of service—meaning which firm can present stronger caliber candidates and expand the services provided, such as behavioral profiling, competitive analysis, and compensation surveys. The best recruiters act as consultants who help their clients' company grow their businesses, rather than just filling certain requisitions.

Our goal is to always expand our services offered, enhance the quality of that service, and expedite the delivery of that service, and achieving all three of those goals can only be possible, in my opinion, if you are not only an expert in the search process, but an active participant in the marketplace that you are recruiting in.

Benchmarking Success

Keeping a search firm on course with respect to generating revenues also involves careful benchmarking. Certainly growth in revenue is a top line benchmark in this industry; retention of recruiters is also absolutely essential, as is acquisition of new recruiters, and finding new industries to serve. Many search organizations fail because they serve only one industry; for example, a search firm that focused on nothing but IT may have grown by 20 to 40 percent in 1997 to 1999, but that growth would have dropped by 30 to 40 percent in 2001 when the industry bust occurred and technology needs dropped. The effects of that industry bust were compounded by the effects stemming from the 9/11 disaster and the resulting recession, and as a result, half of all search firms went out of business over the next three years, and the number of practitioners and recruiters was cut by as much as 70 percent—largely because many search firms at that time were totally focused on IT.

Following trends is not a way to build a business; for example, a mortgage industry crisis would hurt search firms that only specialize in performing searches in the mortgage industry. Therefore, I believe that it is essential for a search firm to diversify and get involved in many different industries and markets, so that when one market begins to lag you can then focus your energies on other markets. Diversification of search practice areas, along with retention of existing staff and acquisition of new staff, are key best practices for every search firm.

Becoming More Client Focused and Less Label Conscious

One of the most difficult aspects of operating an executive search firm is dealing with the labels that the recruiting world puts on itself. Few people understand the meaning between the many different search terms and categories—executive recruiter; management recruiter; search consultant;

retained recruiter; contingent recruiter; contained or retingent search; contract staffing; temporary staffing; permanent search; and direct hire, to name a few. When you get down to it, all of these search categories and positions serve the same purpose—they are aimed at solving a staffing problem by finding the right person for the need.

Unfortunately, the executive search industry seems to overly focus on drawing these lines of demarcation. One firm may say that it only places C-level people, while another will say it only places mid-management or entry level people; one agency may say that it only places salespeople, while another only places technology people; and some agencies will only do searches on a contingent business, while others work strictly on a retained basis, a contract basis, or a permanent basis.

In my opinion, taking that type of approach to recruiting is like going to a restaurant where the waiter asks, "Do you want chicken?—and by the way, here is why chicken is always the best thing to eat," as opposed to simply asking the customer what they want to eat. Making a recommendation after a thorough needs analysis is totally appropriate as do many conformed waiters. However, making a recommendation and refusing to provide what the customer wants are two very different actions. Consider the example of a client who is facing an urgent staffing challenge—they need to hire a superintendent within sixty days to start construction on a new office building, or they will start losing money. That client also has a less urgent staffing challenge—they will need to replace their COO within the next year, and there is no internal candidate to replace that person as a succession strategy. If you are the retained search firm for that client, and your only answer to their staffing challenge is, "I only work at the senior and executive level—sorry, you need to work with someone else on your superintendent search, we do not handle that," you are not effectively serving that client.

I believe that the services of a retained search firm should be dictated on the basis of the urgent and critical nature of the assignment. Therefore, if filling the superintendent position is an urgent need because the company needs to ensure that the position gets filled in a timely manner, then that is the type of job that should be filled through a retained search relationship, regardless of the level of the position. On the other hand, the assignment to fill the senior level COO position is not urgent; in such a case, it may be better to work for the client on a contingency basis, and if you happen to come across a suitable candidate while searching for other candidates over the next six months, you can let the client know. In this case, the appropriate recruiting solution for a $400,000 COO job may be a contingency search, while the appropriate solution for an $80,000 superintendent job may be a retained search.

However, many traditional blue-chip, retained search firms typically draw their business models along lines that have nothing to do with what is in the best interest of their clients, and that, in my opinion, is a big mistake. I believe that the most important role of any search firm is to become a staffing solutions provider, much like a chef who is able to prepare whatever the customer wants to eat. If you cannot meet the client's needs because you do not have anyone on your staff who has the expertise to work on a particular search, then it is logical to turn the client down, but if you have the expertise to work on the client's search, and you know the industry, but you believe that you cannot work on a certain level of search or under certain terms, then you are not running a client-focused search firm.

Being a client-focused search firm is the essence of how we position ourselves in this industry. We believe in being flexible in terms of working with each client to operate around their unique individual needs and expectations on every given search. Not only does every client have different needs, every search requires a different solution. Therefore, in order to really succeed in this field you must be flexible enough to customize your process, your working relationship, and the terms of your agreement around the unique needs of every client. Only then can you truly consider yourself to be a client-focused search firm—there is no "one size fits all" in this field.

Lack of Consolidation and Aggregation

The executive search industry is a very cottage-like industry in that there are very few firms with revenues of more than $100 million. For example, the tenth largest retained search firm according to Executive Search Review is an $18 million firm (us-Kaye/Bassman International), and there is a precipitous drop-off after the next ten listings. In the mid-management recruiting space, Management Recruiters International has a few percent market share with over 1,000 offices, has but a few recruiters in each office, and their number one office is under $10 million in search fee revenue. This organization, by the way, is one of the strongest in their space. Indeed, this industry is so highly fragmented because firms have difficulty in retaining recruiters once they are trained, and there are so few barriers to entry— almost anyone with a telephone can hang up their shingle and call themselves a recruiter. The challenge that our industry is going to face in the years to come is finding a way to put the same type of organization-wide, structural, and systemic efforts that many other more advanced industries have put in place in order to help them grow and expand. The legal industry, for example, has many solo practitioners and small boutiques, but also boasts many firms across all specialty areas and virtually all major geographic markets both domestic and international. These same sized firms can also be found in consulting firms, finance and accounting firms, and virtually every other professional services organization. With respect to the recruiting industry, that is going to require bringing together all of the best practices of many professional services firms in order to promote consolidation, as opposed to the current climate of 16,000 separate search firms—most of which employ fewer than four people. Without larger and multifaceted organizations there can be little aggregation of talent, data, and capabilities. This is not in the best interest of a client seeking to establish a few strategic staffing partners as opposed to dozens on a "vendor" list.

Recent Changes and Future Trends

The search industry was a relatively unknown entity back in the early 1990s; few people understood the concept of executive search at that time. Shortly after that period, however, the idea of core competencies took hold, in that if a certain area was not within the sphere of the organization's core competency, then it should be outsourced to another organization where it is. As companies began to realize that their most precious asset was their people, they increased their usage of outside professionals to assist in securing the best and brightest. As such, one of the many things that began to be outsourced was hiring. As a result, the search industry grew from a $2 billion industry in 1990 to a $10 billion industry in 2000, and as more companies began to outsource their hiring process, our industry kept growing.

These days, not only are clients looking for search firms that have competencies in the area of search, they want search firms that are experts in certain markets and industries—search firms who can act more like staffing partners than staffing vendors. Indeed, in the years to come I believe that we will see fewer staffing agency vendor agreements; rather, we will see many companies that are developing long-term, collaborative, preferred partnerships with a few search organizations that really know their business, their industry, their market, their geography, and their players well enough to be effective in representing their client's interests.

However, the primary focus behind our industry is likely to remain unchanged. Whether you call candidates people or human capital, whether you call yourself a talent acquisition strategist or a headhunter, the words may change, but the concepts behind them do not.

Future Growth Areas

One of the biggest trends that the search industry will be facing in the years to come involves the approaching retirement of millions of baby boomers—and the fact that there are not enough busters coming up to replace them. From 1945 to 1962, 73 million people were born; however, from 1963 to 1980 only 42 million people were born; therefore, the current talent shortage is going to get much worse. There is going to be an across the board staffing shortage in this country, which is why globalization is so important—companies that cannot find enough talent in this country will be forced to look elsewhere, or they will not be able to grow. At the same time, wages may rise to meet the demands of the remaining talent in the marketplace, which may lead to wage inflation in some areas, and this can have a negative effect on the economy overall.

Naturally, the biggest growth industries in the years to come will be those that serve the retiring boomers—wealth management, including banking, insurance, retirement and financial planning services; health care related enterprises such as hospitals, pharmaceutical companies, and long-term living facilities; and the travel and hospitality industry. Technology will be another huge growth area and the race for alternative fuels is likely to spawn a start-up industry in the green energy space. Employment in those fields, along with financial services, health care, and travel, are likely to provide the biggest and brightest opportunities for workers and search firms in the years to come. Areas such as consumer products, hospitality, and retail are also more likely to rise as consumers acquire more disposable income.

Final Thoughts

Our search firm was voted the best company to work for in the state of Texas two years in a row; the best company to work for in the Dallas/Fort Worth area three years in a row; and we are now the largest single site search firm in the country. What those statistics really represent is the fact that we have created a workplace where people are inspired to do great work, and a place where people feel as if they can create long-term opportunities for themselves and their families. If you can create a workplace where people are inspired and driven to work and achieve, rather than a workplace where people feel as if they have to work, you will wind up promoting many positive things: innovation, growth, increased revenues, increased profitability, and longevity in your given industry. Indeed, during the years 2001 to 2004 when most search firms were failing, our firm grew by 10 percent, and we have achieved a 30 percent annual growth rate, on average, for over a decade, and all through organic growth.

In the years to come, I believe that the growth of the search industry is going to be predicated on one key concept: the recruiters that you hire and retain are internal clients that need to be served—they are not employees that need to be managed. If you treat your recruiters like employees, they will leave and go to another firm, or they will start their own business. However, if you help your recruiters feel as if they are your internal clients because they are achieving better personal, professional, and financial growth in your working environment than they could anywhere else, then you will create the kind of great workplace where people will want to stay— and that will translate to benefits for your external clients as well. When you are able to retain a good team of recruiters with long-term experience, you are able to provide a search service with greater levels of depth, consistency, experience, and success. If you do not have a team of tenured, good quality practitioners in your own firm, how can you profess to be able to find such staff members for your clients?

Whenever I speak with other search firms, I will ask, "How long have you been around, and who are your top ten most tenured employees?" If most of the recruiters have been with the firm for five years or less, then I know that the leaders of that search firm are most likely doing some things wrong. You cannot present yourself as an expert in terms of recruiting and retaining candidates if you cannot do these effectively in one's own organization. Therefore, when I consider the tenure of recruiters at a given search firm, that statistic typically tells me which organizations will grow and which will not. Providing a workplace that inspires people to achieve their full potential is critical. We have won awards for workplace flexibility, community service, education, and growth. All are simply reflections of creating an environment where every person "gets" to go to work rather than "has" to go to work. Our executive recruiting firm, through our Next Level Recruiting Training organization, offers a two-day workshop that educates other search firms on how to grow their search businesses. We teach them how to hire, train, and develop a staff of quality recruiters, and how to create a culture that will inspire and retain them. I believe that if more search firms start to follow these best practices, it will create a road map that will enable more firms in this field to scale, and we will end up with many $10+ million search firms, as opposed to only a handful. This is beneficial to clients of search firms, search firm owners, leaders, and producers. Creating a "Next Level" search firm is a continuous journey fraught with successes and "opportunities" to learn. The challenge and reward is in the journey itself.

Jeff Kaye is the chief executive officer of Kaye/Bassman International and newly formed Next Level Recruiting Training. He is also a former Management Recruiters International (MRI) National "Recruiter of the Year." During his tenure as CEO, Kaye/Bassman International has grown into the largest single-site search firm in the country with annual search revenues in excess of $18 million, won national awards for philanthropy and workplace flexibility, and has been named the #1 "Best Company to Work for in Texas" in 2005, 2006, and 2007. He is considered an industry expert in executive, professional and technical search; has appeared on CNN, FOX, Bloomberg, and NBC; and has been quoted in quoted in USA Today, The Wall Street Journal,

Business Week, Time, and Fortune. Jeff has also been a keynote speaker within the staffing community and featured in dozens of national training meetings and videos. He graduated from the University of Texas at Austin with a Bachelor in Business Administration and currently lives in Dallas with his wife and three children.

Successful Searches: Finding the Right Candidate for the Job

Brian D. Thaler

President

Scott-Thaler Associates Agency Inc.

Companies need to recruit talent and expertise for various reasons—they may wish to grow and expand their business; they may need skilled employees to help them solve internal problems; they may have problems retaining their present staff; or their recruiting needs may be a combination of all of those factors. Although a company may be able to recruit new employees by running ads, I believe that in order to find the best talent in a given field, you need to do direct recruiting—i.e., recruit executives from competent companies in your industry.

Executive recruiting is the art of finding qualified people to fill a company's needs. In many cases, companies do not know exactly what type of employees they need to hire, and that is where a skilled executive recruiter steps in. He or she will take the time to really understand what type of expertise the company needs; what the chemistry of the workplace is like; and what the company's objectives and goals are, in order to find the perfect employee-company match.

Recruiting Strategies

In order to find highly qualified candidates for our client companies, our executive recruiting agency considers many facets of each prospective hire: their short- and long-range goals; the financial package they are seeking; how much job-related travel they are willing do; where they are presently located, and whether they are willing to relocate; their energy level; and their personality type. At the same time, we also consider whether our client company will be a good match for the type of expertise, personality, and energy that this candidate offers, and if they are willing to offer the type of compensation and opportunities that the candidate requires.

We want the client to be committed and take ownership for the search assignment. If we find the client company a qualified candidate, we will then work on a retainer or contingency basis. We prefer to work on a retainer basis, in which the client pays us some money up front and the balance upon completion of the assignment; indeed, we very rarely do contingency work, where we are paid only when we finish the project.

A Leadership Plan for the Recruiting Business

Our company's leadership plan is primarily based on enhancing our firm's visibility in the industry; providing quality service for our clients; and serving and managing the interests of our candidates. The premise behind this plan is what I call our "triple win" theory; simply stated, I believe that in order for our recruiting efforts to succeed, the "Candidate, Client, and Recruiter" must all work together as a team.

As an executive recruiter, I believe that it is essential to fully understand what our clients need; what the qualifications of our candidates are; where to find the right candidates; and how to qualify the right candidates. Executive recruiting is not about simply running an ad, sending resumes to the client, and letting them pick who they want to hire. You need to meet with prospective job candidates in person, or screen them thoroughly over the phone, in order to find those candidates who are properly qualified for the client's situation.

Many of our clients do not know exactly what type of employee they need to hire in terms of qualifications; they may just give us a vague job title. In those cases, we act as consultants in that we will actually visit and evaluate the client's facilities and meet key personnel. We have a "Client Needs Analysis" sheet with sixty-six questions. In order to ensure that we meet our client's needs, we also ask prospective candidates to fill out questionnaires aimed at helping us to understand what they are capable of doing, and what they have succeeded in doing in the past—we have about twenty-six questions on our questionnaire regarding this. Our ultimate goal is to take control of both the client and the candidate in terms of getting both parties on the same page. We want each party to be fully aware of what the other party is capable of performing and committing to.

Far too many companies hire an employee after a brief thirty-minute interview, and then put them to work without sufficient training and direction—and all too often, the candidate fails in their new position. Our company's leadership plan is aimed at making sure that each of our candidates is fully aware of the client's goals and expectations in terms of their abilities and capabilities. If a candidate is overqualified for a certain position, he is likely to fail; and if the company is not ready and willing to work with the candidate to help him or her succeed, they will fail to successfully fill their target goals.

Industry Expertise: Meeting the Client's Goals

Fortunately, our interviewing and screening process enables us to find the best candidates for our clients' needs. Our recruiting staff, most of whom have extensive backgrounds in this industry, is trained in understanding every dimension of our candidates' and clients' needs. They receive about two weeks of group and one-to-one training. I train many of my staff people directly, and in order to improve my own recruiting skills, I receive input from some of my staff people as well in how to control the candidate and client at all times. We send our recruiters to get certification with California Staffing Professionals on California staffing laws and ethics. Our senior recruiters hold certified staffing designation and are certified on the national level by the American Staffing Association.

Our staff's collective tenure, experience, and understanding of the industry enable us to successfully evaluate each candidate's ability, and we know how to obtain proper references. After twenty-seven years in this business, we know who to call and who not to call; for example, if a company's HR department will not provide us with references, we know which personnel directors, VPs, or presidents will give us the proper references that we need to obtain in order to find qualified candidates.

Over the years, we have learned from our errors and therefore we are now highly successful at what we do. Whenever we make a mistake, we use form control and better training to correct it for the next time. We feel that it is also important to constantly expand our knowledge base. For example, I recently hired someone to help us understand the aging process as it applies to both businesses and candidates. Studies show that as companies and employees age, they either become smarter, or they get locked into a state of mind where they cannot see the whole picture, and we want to learn how to deal with that situation.

Our agency specializes in hiring executives for the fashion industry. My knowledge base in that area is extensive—I am president of the Textile Association of Los Angeles; I am also on the board of the California

Fashion Association; and I am an active member of Fashion Bureau Inc. In addition to my membership in the leading fashion trade organizations, I go to all the industry shows. Our agency lives and breathes this industry, which has contributed greatly to our success in meeting our clients' goals.

Meeting with Clients and Screening Candidates

Whenever we first meet with a new client, we will ask its representatives at least sixty-six questions in order to obtain full background information about the company and the position that is being offered, and we want to know all about the people in the organization who will be working with our candidate. We also like to see the physical layout of the company; and if the company has stores, we will visit them as well. We want to understand every single factor and facet pertaining to the company and the personalities who work there and we want to get a feel for the energy, direction, and pulse of that company, and how they represent themselves in the industry.

Next, we start looking for qualified candidates that fit the client's profile and can achieve the objectives that the company is looking for. We look at our database for candidates, we do direct recruiting, networking, attend and participate in trade shows, and work through referrals. We always give the client a full report on each candidate we have screened and we will not send them anyone who we do not think is a good fit for their company. Each of our candidates is well qualified for the job they are interviewing for.

I also help clients adjust their hiring requirements when necessary. For example, one of our clients wished to hire one executive to fill a $250,000 position. In this instance, I persuaded the client to hire two separate executives, each at a salary of $125,000, because I felt that one person would not be able to do what the client was looking for. The client wanted a marketing and sales manager. We found them one person specializing in sales and one in marketing. They would then work as a team and accomplish the company's goals.

Meeting Challenges

Two of the biggest challenges that recruiters face in this industry are retaining qualified candidates who receive counteroffers from other recruiters—no recruiter wants to lose good candidates—and client apathy, i.e., a client who cannot make a decision, and therefore needlessly prolongs the hiring process.

In order to overcome these two situations, we train our recruiters on how to pre-qualify a counteroffer. This entails asking their candidates many times how they feel about a counteroffer and what their current company policy is regarding counteroffers. I always make sure that the client is aware that they have to move extremely fast in terms of making an offer or they may wind up losing their momentum in the hiring process—and losing the candidate. I try to mentor and work with the client throughout the hiring process, and if they are apathetic I will let them know that they are wasting my time, and may be missing out on a good candidate.

The Value of Successful Recruiting

We add financial value to our client companies, and to our own, by finding candidates who are well qualified to achieve our clients' business goals. We also recommend that our clients properly position the candidate to hit the ground running by giving them a detailed job description which includes their mission statement, and what they want the candidate to achieve. In addition, we make sure that our clients properly introduce their new hires to the peer staff members they will be working with; the people they will report to; and the people they will supervise.

I always call my clients after the hiring process is complete in order to review how they felt about the process, and I will continue to check in with them for a couple of months to see how the candidate is doing. Similarly, I will stay in contact with the candidate to see how they are doing on the job, and if there are any problems, we will try to play the middleman and work things out. We call the candidate at least seven times within a three month period to see how they are doing. We also call the client to see how our candidate is performing. We usually solve problems and concerns through good follow-up and communication.

Gaining Market Share: Dealing with the Competition

We have found that the best way to gain market share in this industry is to do a better job and provide better service than our competitors and work to increase our visibility. The key to closing a search is having the best qualified candidates.

Fortunately, we have found that once a client works with our agency they never want to leave us, because we always find good candidates. Many of our clients are shocked when they discover the extent of our industry knowledge, compared to that of most other recruiting agencies. Our clients are typically very comfortable in working with our recruiters and they ultimately find that we can give them better results than our competitors are able to achieve. I also keep our clients in the loop of what is happening in the industry, and I invite them to the many textile and apparel functions that I am involved in.

Generally speaking, competition is good for our company although it can hurt us at times. If we are working a search that three other search firms are working, we can be stepping on each others' toes by recruiting the same candidates. However, it often helps us as well, because when our competitors do not do a good job, we are likely to be in greater demand.

The Importance of Client Service

Indeed, providing top quality client service is a key element in the success of any recruiting agency. In order to serve our clients most successfully, we work directly with their top decision makers and interviewing staff. We like to do our job right the first time by taking the time to fully understand who the client is and what they are looking for. If we know what the client company is all about and what they represent, and what the personality of the company is like and what they are looking for in a candidate, we can then better match the client to a candidate. Understanding the client's needs also enables us to properly advise them after the hiring process is complete. We explain how they can best benefit from their new hire's skill sets—i.e., how to use those skills to achieve their corporate goals.

Recruiting agencies that fail to provide top-notch client service typically do not understand their clients and candidates to the fullest extent, and in many cases, they do not deal honestly with their clients. For example, if I am also sending a candidate to three of the client's competitors in addition to the client company, I will make sure that my client is aware of that fact. It is also essential to properly follow through with respect to all of the phases, and we have creative steps of recruiting.

Overcoming Difficulties

Whenever I run into a difficult situation with one of our clients, I always remind them that I am not here to hurt them, but to help them. I let them know that my staff is trained and motivated to fulfill their needs, and if we have a problem, we can work it out. If a client and a candidate run into problems after the hiring process is complete, we help them work through their difficulties.

A friend of mine who is the director of Fashion Bureau Inc. has inspired the industry by teaching its leaders what to do with their lives and careers, and that is what we try to offer our clients and candidates. In many cases, we need to guide both parties through the hiring process; and that process may entail telling the candidate how to dress for an interview, or advising a client on how to conduct an interview, and the importance of making an offer in a timely manner. It is often important to stand up to your clients and candidates and take control of the hiring process. If you let the candidate and client try to work things out, in most cases many things could work against you. The middleman can represent both parties without them antagonizing each other. You also need to know what is going on in the industry at all times.

Advising Recruiters, Clients, and Candidates

One of the biggest challenges of working in this industry is dealing with rejection. In addition, many recruiters fail at this job because they refuse to take responsibility for their actions, and they blame the failure of the search on the candidate or the client. I train my recruiters on how to deal with failure and avoid mistakes.

I also make my clients and candidates aware of the shortcomings and realities of the recruiting process. For example, if I send four candidates out on a job interview, the reality is that the candidate who is likely to get the position is the one who has paid attention to what the recruiter told them about the client and how to represent themselves to the client. If the client asks me which candidate I think they should hire, I will tell them the pros and the cons of every candidate I sent them, but I will not make that decision for them.

Taking Control

Taking control of the recruiting process is essential, and succeeding in that effort entails having compassion for the people you are dealing with and being a good listener. For example, about fifteen years ago, one of my candidates accepted a position, and then suddenly changed his mind. In order to find out why, I called his house when I knew he was not home in order to speak to his wife. It turned out that she did not want him to take the job because it would mean that they would have to move to California, and she was afraid that their prize-winning Afghan hound would die from flea and tick bites if they moved to that state.

Twenty minutes later, I had the director of the Afghan Hound Company in Los Angeles call the woman and convince her that if she brought her dog to California it would not be adversely affected by fleas and ticks, and indeed, it would probably win more contests in California than in New York. She ultimately convinced her husband to take the job. Therefore, it is often essential to dig deep in order to reassert control in the recruiting process.

Service with a Difference

Nearly every recruiting company is now computer-based and has its own Web site. We are able to contact our candidates through various means of technology. We are also able to better grow our network and contacts; therefore, it is increasingly essential in today's fast-paced business world to offer personalized knowledgeable service which helps you stand out in the crowd.

Our firm focuses on offering the right service for each of our clients and candidates. We know how to immediately steer our clients to the right candidates, and if a candidate needs a new position, we can quickly steer them to the right employer. We do not look for jobs for candidates; we look for careers for our candidates. Similarly, we do not look for candidates; we look for potential junior partners who will be committed and loyal to the client company.

Taking the time to understand your client and your candidate, while moving along the hiring process in a timely manner, can be challenging, but if a candidate is ready to make a move, and so is the client, you may have to move extremely fast in order to ensure that a match is made. When you start doing references on some of the candidates, references would be surprised the candidate is looking for a career change and may call them up directly and offer them a position with their company.

No matter how much the industry may change in the years to come, we believe that the essential ingredients for success in recruiting remain constant. Understanding the industry and offering good service to candidates and clients is essential, as is being active and visible in the industry and supporting its efforts. If you do not love and actively support the industry that you are in, you will ultimately fail at what you do.

Brian D. Thaler began his twenty-eight year career in the retail industry with Lerner's Dress Shops in New York, which was the beginning to a successful progression within merchandise administration. Mr. Thaler was general merchandise administrator for the entire Franklin Simon Dept. Stores Co., G.M.A. for the Weiner Corp., and merchandise controller for Fashion Conspiracy.

During this period in his career, Mr. Thaler identified a pronounced lack of employee expertise in the retail industry. In light of this realization, he joined an executive consulting/search firm as vice president. This gave him the opportunity to use his acquired knowledge and contacts of seventeen years to assist specialty retailers with their staffing needs. Mr. Thaler was also able to facilitate the implementation of policies and procedures within company's traffic and physical distribution operations.

Shortly thereafter, Mr. Thaler started Scott-Thaler Associates. His professional, ethical, and confidential approach to the field of executive search has been the success of Scott-Thaler Associates. Since STA's founding, we have established networks with top professionals in our specialty divisions of apparel, textiles, freight forwarding, retail, supply chain management, and management consulting.

One of the most important philosophies Mr. Thaler has created through his years of being in the fashion and the executive search industry is the "Triple Win" philosophy. The "Triple Win" occurs when client, candidate, and recruiter work together and through their synergy, place the right person in the right position under the right circumstances. The client, candidate, and recruiter all win.

Mr. Thaler is the president of the Textile Association of Los Angeles and has been on the board of directors for over five years. He is also currently a member of the California Fashion Association and Fashion Business, Inc. Mr. Thaler is a past president of the California Association of Personnel Consultants and has been involved in the CAPC and CSP for many years.

The Recruiter as a Sherpa: Helping Your Clients Make the Right Hire

David S. Harap

Partner-Global Practice Leader

Stanton Chase International

The role of an executive recruiter entails acting as a consultant to your clients in terms of helping them to identify, assess, and recruit specific senior level executives to their organization. Our search firm serves a wide array of clients, from very early stage start-ups to Fortune 50 companies in a diverse range of industries. After assessing the client's needs, we help them to identify what kind of candidates they are looking for—what backgrounds, cultures, and executive leadership styles would result in the most suitable fit and have the most impact on their organization.

Next, we identify specific candidates and we determine how to reach out to them in the marketplace, bring them to the table, and get them interested in the client's opportunity. It is essential to fully assess the candidate's skills, and then manage and coordinate the entire recruitment process with the client until the candidate is successfully on board.

A Unique Search Focus: Profit-Building Strategies

Each of our recruiter consultants specializes in just one or two industries; however, we recruit for most industries and most positions, from senior directors up through CEOs and board members. The market niche that we pride ourselves on filling is based on our entrepreneurial focus—we are highly nimble and responsive to the client's needs. Fortunately, we have the flexibility and speed of a boutique firm, but we also have the breadth of one of the world's ten largest search firms.

Many of our clients come to us in part because of our global capabilities; for example, we can put together a seamless global solution for those clients that are looking to grow or recruit from the Asian Pacific region and Eastern Europe, which are two of the fastest growing markets. Indeed, one of the primary strengths of our firm is our ability to conduct searches for global clients thanks to our widespread network of consultants, some of whom are based here while others are based in Asia and Europe. Each client has one local contact person, but supporting that person is a global team.

Another unique aspect of our search process is that we always look for ways to proactively add value to our client company, and that involves not only presenting them with eight or twelve great candidates, but also providing them with market intelligence and compensation information—any information that is relevant to how the client is perceived in the marketplace. For example, during the course of a search we will reach out to 150 to 200 potential candidates, and we will try to pull together data points that we assemble during that process and feed them back to the client in a meaningful way. We collect data such as compensation, equity participation, perception of the client in the market, etc., to feed back to the client. We believe in adding value to the client company by utilizing strategies that go far beyond compiling resumes and such value-added service builds client loyalty—and helps us to achieve long-term profits.

We also look to build profits through our visibility at industry conferences and trade shows. We try to be where our clients and candidates are—we want to be viewed as an integral player in our clients' specific industries. Our clients are looking for consultants and search firms who can truly be an extension of their businesses. They do not want to pay a search firm who needs to learn about their industry; they want to work with consultants who already know their business, know the players in their business, and are able to attract candidates that they would not normally have access to. No one is going to retain an executive search firm to identify candidates who are in transition, or the type of candidates who would be replying to an ad on Monster.com.

Balancing Short- and Long-Term Goals

In order to set short- and long-term goals for our search firm, we conduct global meetings on a twice yearly basis. I believe that it is always much more effective to set short- and long-term strategies in a face-to-face environment, especially because we are often dealing with searches that cut across so many offices, countries, and cultures. Face-to-face meetings allow the consultants to put their thoughts on the table, and help ensure that everyone is equally committed to our short- and long-term goals. However, balancing those two types of goals is always challenging; while you want to achieve short-term results, you also need to implement the long-term planning and investment strategies that go into creating a sustainable and growing business.

Our goals are always client-focused; for example, we are currently looking to develop a collection of truly global client firms and serve them effectively in all four regions where our company operates. Our biggest challenge lies in knowing when we are not succeeding in our efforts—i.e., knowing when we need to remove a certain client from our target list and move on. Our general rule of thumb is that if we are not satisfied with our progress after twenty-four months, then we need to forget about that potential client.

Working with New Clients: Analyzing the Client's Culture

The most important thing that we always do at the beginning of a new candidate search is to spend time with the client. We walk the halls of the client company and try to meet as many people as we can; in addition to meeting with the entire management team we try to spend time with people at all levels of the client's organization, because that is the only way to get a real feel for the client's culture, and what kind of person would thrive in that environment.

The first search for a new client is always the most challenging, because it is a learning process. By the time you have conducted a second or third search for the same client company you have generally developed a strong intuition with respect to which candidate would make a good cultural fit for that company's culture, but the first search can be more challenging—and the best way to meet that challenge is to invest a lot of time in visiting and communicating with the client company.

The Candidate Search: The Reference Checking Process

The process of narrowing down a candidate search is typically driven by spending about two hours with each candidate in a face-to-face interview—and trusting your intuition. However, even if your intuition tells you that a certain person would be a great fit for your client's company—or conversely, even if your intuition tells you that a candidate with an impressive track record would not be a good fit for the client's team—it is always essential to document and articulate that instinct through a comprehensive written candidate assessment that the client can read and appreciate. The assessment allows the candidate's achievements and responsibilities to be put in proper context.

Creating that assessment is usually the result of an extensive reference checking process. However, reference checking can be a challenge, because while you would like to talk to twenty different references for each candidate, almost all of our candidates are gainfully employed; therefore you have to be discreet and mindful of the legal boundaries that are involved in terms of conducting reference checks. Our reference checking can never jeopardize the candidate's current employment. Nevertheless, we always try to interview a minimum of eight to ten references for each candidate. Many search consultants do not push as hard as we do in this area because they do not want to uncover any challenges or gray areas. However, we believe that extensive reference checking is essential in order to determine if someone is truly a viable candidate—and if not, you have to keep recruiting.

Indeed, we believe that you are doing your clients a disservice if you do a superficial reference check; therefore, we always spend a lot of time and effort on conducting very thorough reference checks, including verification of the candidate's education and any kind of accreditation that they are claiming.

A Typical Candidate Search

As an example of a typical candidate search, a new CEO came on board at one of our client companies, and he wanted to change the HR organization by recruiting a VP of HR who would report directly to him. The incumbent was a long-term employee who was at the director level, and the client decided that until he had a chance to talk with that individual he wanted the search to be conducted in the strictest of confidence.

I subsequently spent about six hours with that CEO, getting to know his style and listening to his vision with respect to where his company was going and what challenges they would be facing in the years to come. Therefore, I was able to gain an understanding of the challenges that the person coming into this VP of HR role would face, not only over the next six months, but also the challenges that they would be facing three years out.

As a result of this interviewing process, I was able to craft a position description, which I sent back to the CEO in order to get his opinion of my efforts. That job description ultimately went through three or four different drafts, and when that process was finally complete we were able to start recruiting. We ultimately talked with 150 people for the client's position, taking care to keep the client's search information confidential throughout the initial screening process.

I then returned to the client and together we reviewed the backgrounds of the twelve strongest candidates. Next, we narrowed that field down to eight candidates, and I am now in the process of conducting extensive face-to-face interviews with these finalists in order to choose the three top candidates who I feel will make the strongest contribution to the client's organization, and who would represent the best cultural fit in terms of their ability to work effectively with the client and his management team.

Challenges of Finding the Right Candidate

One of the biggest challenges of working on this assignment is the fact that it is my first search for this client; therefore, I am still getting to know this CEO's style, and I am still learning what kind of executives would work well with him. This is a company that is poised to go through explosive growth; therefore, we need to find a candidate who is able to buy into the client's vision and growth strategies. He or she needs to understand that this job will represent an amazing career opportunity in the years to come; therefore, our challenge involves not just selling a vision with respect to what the job consists of at the present time, but what that job will look like a few years from now.

Indeed, although we have developed a great slate of candidates for this client, the challenge lies in getting those candidates to look at the client's opportunity in the broadest possible terms. We need to help the candidates look past their initial reaction to the client's job description; we need to get them excited about the job's future prospects. If a candidate initially says that they are not interested in the client's position, I may have to call that candidate several times in an effort to change their mind. Good recruiters are always friendly but persistent—and they never accept a "no" answer during a first conversation with a promising candidate.

Growing Revenues and Profits

Our executive search firm has found that the best way to grow our revenues is by continuing to move upstream with our clients—i.e., by filling increasingly senior level positions, and delving ever deeper into the client's organization. If we serve the client in one or two markets, we always try to expand our efforts into five or six markets. If we work with the client in Europe, we will try to serve them in the Asia Pacific area and North America as well.

In order to grow revenues and profits you also have to grow your existing client base. However, although you always want to add new clients, you have to make sure that you keep enough of the industry off limits that you have a lot of fertile recruiting ground, since you cannot recruit from existing clients. Therefore, you have to find the right balance in terms of adding clients, and focus most of your growth strategies around your existing clients by finding new ways to serve them better and move up the food chain with them. One of our clients, a large European technology company, was transforming themselves from a product company to a service company. We provided numerous market intelligence reports at low costs on the DNA of executives from the market segments they were looking to grow in. When they began to build out their new management team, we were a true partner in the process.

Gaining Market Share

The executive search industry is highly competitive in that most clients will talk to two or three search firms before they decide to award an assignment. We have found that the most effective way to compete against other large global firms is by running a very lean and flexible operation that allows us to be very competitive in terms of price. While you never want to win an assignment based solely on price, if everything else is comparable we can certainly be very competitive compared to the pricing strategies used by many other large search firms.

For example, we usually do assignments on a fixed fee basis, as opposed to most search firms that bill clients in one-third installments, with the final invoice based on the actual compensation. We have found that clients really gravitate towards a fixed fee billing system. We are also able to gain market share from the competition because we tend to look for repeat clients who give us multiple assignments.

Improving Client Service and Building Customer Loyalty

Of course, no search firm can be successful unless it offers excellent client service. The best way to build customer loyalty is to always listen to the client—if I am doing most of the talking during a client meeting, then something is terribly wrong. It is also essential to continually look for ways to add value to the search process. Clients naturally assume that we are going to be able to present them with eight to twelve qualified candidates, but how do you go beyond that—how do you provide a broader search solution? That solution may entail making a stronger assessment of the client company in order to find candidates that will represent a better cultural fit; providing compensation data; or helping the client get a feel for what kind of candidates are in the marketplace so that they can benchmark their internal candidates—whatever it takes to help the client make a stronger and better hiring decision.

In order to build trust and loyalty with our clients, we strive to be viewed as an extension of the client's leadership team, and the only way to accomplish that goal is to do a lot of work for the client and spend a lot of time at their company. We always commit the time that is necessary to walk the halls of the client company and build a strong rapport and relationship with their entire leadership team.

I believe that there is only one benchmark for determining whether your client is truly loyal, and that is when they automatically call your search firm when a search opportunity arises, rather than calling three different firms. If the client chooses to work with your firm every time they need to recruit a new executive, then you know that you have a loyal client, and you know that you are serving them well.

Marketing Strategies

Marketing is another important element in a search firm's growth strategies, and the primary goal of any marketing strategy is to increase your visibility in the marketplace. Effective marketing helps in terms of client acquisition, but it also creates brand awareness that can be useful in terms of candidate development. If a candidate recognizes our name, or has worked with one of our consultants in the past, we have instant credibility with that candidate.

Our firm's marketing strategies include advertising in industry and trade journals, as well as sponsorship of industry associations and trade shows. We also market our service by attending critical conferences and symposiums within each industry that we serve, a strategy which increases our visibility in those key industry markets. We look to attend both local/regional conferences as well as the large global events.

Benchmarking

In this business you are only as good as your last search; therefore, we measure our success by our ability to increase the share of our revenue that is coming from repeat clients. If a client is happy with our service, they will continue to give us more business, and I believe that the number of repeat clients is the strongest metric a search firm can have.

One of the other internal metrics that we use to measure our growth is how many referrals are going on within our firm. For example, if a client tells me that they have a recruiting need in India, we will team up our domestic efforts with our office in India. Such teamwork with overseas branches of our company will be critical to our success in the years to come, due to the growing trend of search firms enlisting global teams to serve their clients.

Difficult and Rewarding Aspects of the Recruiting Business

Perhaps the most difficult aspect of working in the executive recruiting industry is the fact that we are dealing with people—executives who may have to relocate with their spouse and children. Therefore, there is a very personal component to what we do. You cannot lose sight of that fact that you are not only dealing with executives and career opportunities—you are dealing with human beings and changing jobs and relocating can mean a major disruption to their lives. When you work in an industry where you are dealing with people, you have to expect many surprises and challenges.

However, executive recruiting can also be a singularly rewarding career. I measure my success by my ability to help everyone in my practice be more successful—are they serving their clients better and doing stronger work? Are their individual business development and revenue targets being met? If I am doing my job well, then everyone who works for me will become more successful as well—and so will our clients and candidates.

The Importance of Innovation

Executive recruiters know that there is never one single solution that is going to fit every client. Therefore, we must be willing to view every search as a unique opportunity; we always try to see if we can serve the client in a new and different way. In each case, it is important to sit down with the client to create a search process that will either serve their specific needs in a better way, or represents a better approach for their specific search—whatever it takes to be successful, because we know that you cannot do every search in the same way.

For example, we recently handled an assignment for a fast-growing client company that had won a major government contract that would allow them to grow from $3 million in revenues to $97 million in revenues in just twelve months. The client, a health care company, had to staff up across two states—they were based in the mid-Atlantic region and the contract they had won involved serving 15,000 patients in the Southeast. Therefore, the client had to build an entire infrastructure to support this new program in real time. I helped the client to recruit the VPs that were needed to support the program, and I also worked with them to build out their entire team.

During the recruiting process, we generated a number of detailed candidate assessments for our client to consider. However, the client told us that they did not have the time to read all of that material, and they asked us to come up with a different approach to the assessment process. Working with the client, we came up with a numeric system for rating the candidates on a scale of one to ten, and if I rated a candidate between seven and ten we would fly them up to interview at the client's corporate office. In this case, the client trusted my judgment to the extent that they did not care to read the six-page assessment I had produced for each candidate—they just wanted to see the candidates who I ranked at a high level. Although I have not used that numeric rating system since that assignment, it was what that particular client wanted and it was an appropriate solution in that situation. Innovation in this industry should always be aimed at serving the client's needs.

Recruiting Industry Trends and Upcoming Growth Areas

Looking at recent trends in the recruiting field, it is easy to see that technology has made a huge impact on what we do. For example, it has greatly accelerated the pace of doing business; clients expect you to be responsive to their needs almost instantaneously—they know you have a Blackberry and they want information in real time.

Technology has also greatly leveled the playing field in this industry. In the past, recruiters used to take pride in having huge, proprietary databases; however, such databases have now become irrelevant. Thanks to the Internet, it is very easy to identify people in a given field, and any database usually becomes stagnant after about one year. Therefore, you are likely to be able to maintain a good database of candidates just by staying active in this industry, but you do not need to focus on assembling a huge proprietary database because you will most likely need to create a custom candidate pool for every single search.

Looking ahead, I believe that global searches will be the biggest growth area in the executive recruiting industry. I believe that more companies will be putting together project and leadership teams irregardless of where the team members are situated; therefore, clients will expect recruiting firms to find the right candidates wherever those individuals may be located. At the present time, about half of my assignments involve simultaneous candidate development in the U.S. and Europe, or Europe and the Asia Pacific region, and I believe that trend will continue to grow.

For example, our firm is now working with a new university in the Middle East that has asked us to recruit their five top provost level positions, and they want at least half of the candidates to come from North America, and the balance to come from either Europe or Australia. In order to serve this project we have put together a global recruiting team, and such assignments are becoming more typical. There are companies in China that want marketing expertise from Europe and North America, and there are companies in India that are looking to grow their presence in North America and build leadership teams here. In the latter case, we need to look for executives in India who want to go to America, and executives in America who may have done their undergraduate studies in India.

Indeed, in order to serve our clients effectively in the years to come we will need to assemble recruiting teams situated across multiple countries and regions. That strategy will add value to our clients' searches; the only drawback, from our standpoint, is those early morning conference calls.

David S. Harap has over eighteen years of experience serving a broad client base as a senior level executive search consultant. Widely recognized as a strategic partner on all of his client engagements, he has been involved in over 275 successful searches, spanning all senior level executive and functional leadership positions.

Prior to joining Stanton Chase, Mr. Harap was a partner with a boutique search firm and a principal with Korn/Ferry International where he was a founding member of the Global Healthcare Products and a core member of the global technology practice, with a focus on emerging technologies within both global practices. During his nine-year tenure with the global firm, Mr. Harap was a critical contributor in establishing their Austin, TX and Princeton, NJ offices. His career in executive search began with a boutique executive search firm with offices in Palo Alto, New York, and London where he was the global research director.

Mr. Harap lectures at the University of Texas at Austin and is also an active member of the Austin Technology Council, Texchange, Nanotechnology Foundation of Texas, and Cornell Alumni Federation board member. Mr. Harap received a B.S. in industrial and labor relations from Cornell University as a Father Kelly Scholar in 1989.

Putting the Focus on Great People, Great Clients, and Great Relationships

Lace Bourgeois Archibald, CTS, CSP, CERS

President

ML&R Personnel Solutions LLC

Executive recruiting is the business of searching for and identifying human talent on behalf of client organizations. Companies engage us to help them build their teams, replace talent that has departed, or to solve unique business problems. It is about your ability to identify and match talent that provides a "best fit" for the client. Talent is identified through multiple sources, but primarily through a recruiter's personal candidate database and extensive networks developed over the years. Once a candidate is employed, search firms are compensated in several ways. The two main fee structures are contingency and retained, and in recent years, a combination of the two. If the fee structure is retained, the client pays a percentage of the fee up front when they engage us to do the search. There are specific deliverables due on a scheduled timeline and additional fee payments are made as deliverables are met. When hired on a contingency basis, no fees are received up front. The search firm only gets paid if, and when, the client hires one of our candidates. In a combined fee structure, the client company pays part of the fee up front, with the remainder due upon placement of the candidate. The fee may or may not be reimbursed depending on contractual agreements. In very recent times, we have started to see some firms provide services on flat fee basis. Typically, these are companies that compete on price and volume, but this is not the norm. There are several challenges the search firm must be aware of when working on a contingency basis. The client may be utilizing multiple search firms so there is a greater risk that your candidate might not be the one selected, resulting in zero revenue. In essence you might be working for free. Second, as there is no financial outlay from the client, there is not the same commitment to the search firm as there would be with a retained search.

The decision to focus on relationships rather than transactions allows us to build a strong client base and grow through repeat business and candidate referrals. We are comfortable with turning away business with companies when we know we cannot build the sort of relationship with them that would be productive for both our company and theirs. This enables us to concentrate our energies on clients that have value systems compatible with our own. The decision to focus on what we do well, and not what our competition does, has allowed us to forge strong alliances both within and outside the search industry. This has led to increased business and allowed us to serve a much broader market than some larger organizations can.

We know that we need to have great people, great clients, and great execution to be successful. While many companies say this, we have adopted this slogan as part of our strategic initiative. Coupled with our mission statement, "We care for our clients, we care for our people," we have established an internal culture that clients recognize as one that makes them feel important and know they have our undivided attention. Personally, as president of the company, I feel very fortunate to hear in the marketplace about how my team provided "great service, and truly took my interests to heart." We began by hiring people to work for us who believe in what we are doing, and who bring skill sets with them that enhance what we are doing. Then we provide them with the tools, training, and work environment to allow them to succeed in their job. This is not without risk, as these people become well trained, and ultimately most are capable of performing the search business on their own. Some in fact have left our company to do just that.

We are selective when choosing our clients. We want to work with people who respect and see value in the services we provide. Our client acceptance model takes into consideration our evaluation of those clients we would enjoy working with and that share a similar value system. Equally as important, we want to work with clients who we believe provide a work environment that a prospective candidate would feel comfortable working in. Contrary to popular belief, you cannot be afraid to say no to a potential client. And remember that if they are only worried about the fee, then in the long run they probably won't be a good client. You may make some money, but by our definition, you won't have a great client.

Maintaining Standards

We believe in great execution. We deliver what we say we will. We strive to exceed the expectation of our customers, both for our clients and our candidates. We take the time to learn what is important to them, do it, and then continue to follow up and invest in building a relationship. Mistakes happen to remind us that we are human. When something does go wrong, we address the situation, we work to fix it, and we continue to build the relationship. Most companies run for cover when something bad happens, we happen to look at it as one of the greatest opportunities to prove we care about our client.

From an industry perspective, I cannot say that we have done anything that is so different, other than executing on our business model. First, our ability to develop an extensive network of professionals has provided us the opportunity to excel in delivering talent to the marketplace. Second, we utilize a consultative model in delivering service to the clients. Our primary objective is to assist our clients in solving their business problems. In situations where we are searching for a person to replace a non performing individual, we find that it is not always a human capital problem that actually needs resolving. Instead it may be a business process issue, departmental competency, technology or even a moral issue that needs to be addressed. If we identify that this is the case, then we look to provide real solutions to fix these issues before we assist them in hiring talent. For example, we had placed several individuals with one of our larger clients. About six months into their tenure, we started getting calls sharing with us that they were unhappy and wanted to possibly look for new opportunities. Wearing a consultative hat, we probed to determine what was causing the dissatisfaction. We learned that the company, due to some rapid growth, had recently promoted several employees into supervisory roles. Following up with a senior executive of the company, we determined that these new supervisors had received minimal training. This made it difficult for the candidates, but more importantly, set the new managers up for potential failure. Meeting with the CFO and other managers, we discussed the potential turnover issues, and ultimately, the retention risk of his current staff. The ultimate solution was not to continue hiring individuals, but to develop a comprehensive training program for the affected managers. He brought in training and our proactive consultation resulted in him retaining all of his staff.

We strive to be a strategic partner with our clients, not just another vendor. We learn all we can about our client company, their goals, strategic plans, and their future staffing requirements; we work to build a strong relationship so they see our firm as the place to go when they have human capital questions. We want to be viewed as the company that can provide unique solutions to their problems. In order to do this successfully, it is imperative that we develop a strong network of strategic alliances. This allows us to bring a variety of solutions to the table that will address their specific business issues and requirements. By adopting this approach, we provide our client with options that allow them to utilize their extensive knowledge to choose the best available option.

When a prospective client comes to us, we begin by investigating their business problem through inquiry and discussion with them. If we think we can provide a solution then we explain our process, discuss our fees, and if these are acceptable to them, we set up our first meeting. During this meeting we explore the company's requirements, corporate culture, and business environment. Through this process we gain greater insight into their problem and the environment the candidate will be going into.

We evaluate candidates on a variety of factors while insuring that we prescribe to the same EEOC (Equal Employment Opportunity Commission) requirements as other hiring entities. We look at the candidate's education, work experience, skill sets, competencies, and other factors, then we assess how well they match the requirements outlined in our initial and follow-up discussions. We continue to refine our search as the interview process progresses to ensure we will find the candidate that will be a good fit both technically and culturally in the organization. Then we arrange for an interview between our client and our candidate. It goes without saying that the decision to hire rests with our client company.

We assess our candidates with an in-depth interview comprised of multiple types of questions designed to evaluate skills, experience, and behaviors. In addition, we perform reference checks with the candidate's peers, subordinates, and supervisors in order to gain insight on their past history and performance. Sometimes our client will ask us to use personality or skill assessments such as Insights and Birkman to assist them in making their candidate selections.

In our business, our candidate's references are especially important. We have a process in place that we follow with regards to reference checking. When we meet candidates we request three peer, three subordinate, and three supervisor references who we can contact. We also have them sign a release allowing us permission to check and release the information we gather. We have specific questions designed to provide insight on their performance, skill sets, work ethic, and management styles, and we request they describe situations that could set our candidate up for success or failure. This tool gives us a fair insight into our candidate's strengths and abilities.

Our greatest challenge is matching up our client's goals for a candidate, with the candidate's goals for a career. Very seldom do the cover letters and résumés that job seekers compose accurately reflect their skills and accomplishments. Some tend to overstate the breadth and depth of their experience, while others undersell their skills. The search team has to analyze both situations to uncover the truth in order to place the right person in the right position. These search skills are the reason you sometimes hear clients say it is like finding a diamond in the rough. The second challenge is career management. In reality, only a small proportion of individuals have taken the time to map out their careers, and then executed plans to achieve their goals. While many things change, the candidate who has at least thought about his career path is much easier to work with than the ones who have not. For the majority of candidates, we need more time just to determine if they would be a good fit. Many companies in the search business are not concerned about the long-term fit of a candidate, so they don't invest the time to give career guidance.

For the person just starting their professional employment, partnering with an executive recruiter can help the employee determine if the position is right for him relative to other opportunities in the marketplace. For employees seeking to change careers, the skills of a good recruiter can help the employee understand some of their internal drivers to focus them on the right position for them. The risk of not doing this is that careers are derailed because the employee took a position that in the end wasn't right for them, and did not contribute to them reaching their career goals.

Generating Revenue

We base our fees on a percentage of the successful candidate's first year's annualized compensation. Our fees are standard across the board. We do offer a special rate when we provide our services to charitable and nonprofit organizations as this is our way to give back and contribute to our community.

We strive to deliver what we promise. We provide quality candidates who meet the hiring requirements and solve the business challenges of our clients. We work both independently and as a team, always keeping in mind that our job is to identify the best candidate for our client's position. This results in a high percentage of repeat business and referrals.

We maintain ongoing communication with our clients and candidates so that we can eliminate any nasty surprises for anyone concerned. Some people might say we spend too much time communicating, but in our business communication pays dividends.

We care for our people and provide them with a work environment that gives them flexibility and the tools they need to do their jobs well.

We have no strategy for taking away market share from any of our competitors. We stay true to our core values and have found that by providing quality services, business comes to us. We provide consistent delivery of quality service. We communicate and return our calls. We are persistent in our follow-up and make sure they have resolved their business problems. Ultimately a company wants to hire the best talent, so we make sure we are well networked and have talent to present when they call for assistance.

We approach each client individually understanding that they each have unique problems and requirements. There are many firms that provide standard solutions for a client's problems, but that doesn't work for firms such as ours that have a business model built around a consultative approach. We take the time to get to know them and ask how they would like to be serviced. No matter how well a company performs, you can never assume that how you do it is going to be right for that specific client. We avoid providing our clients with quick answers we think they want to hear. When we make a mistake we do what we can to fix it, not just ignore it and hope it will go away. We continuously keep in mind that it is a privilege to do business with them and strive to be viewed as a business partner.

The executive recruiter is in a unique position to be a business partner with both the client firms and the executive candidates. We genuinely care for our customers and take an interest in their companies not only when they need our help but also when they do not need us. We are an advocate for our clients, and promote their business with referrals when we identify another company that could utilize their services or products. Just as important, we care about our candidates and assisting them in their career decisions. Great candidate networks are only developed through genuine consideration of the candidate's goals and career aspirations. We are an advocate for the candidate when we find the right position, just as we are an advocate for the client in promoting their products and services.

Marketing Strategy

Obviously marketing is important and letting people know about you, your company, and the services you offer is critical. We find our best marketing is done by the clients and candidates we have worked with, and have experienced firsthand our approach to executive search. They know that how we work is different and results in a positive experience. Over time we have discovered that people share with other people. They tell others of their experiences, and they are our best advertisers. In addition, we are involved in the community, industry groups, and networking. We find that word-of-mouth and networking have a much greater impact than the traditional methods of advertising.

We listen to our clients and candidates, we evaluate their feedback, and we implement changes to our process and procedures when that is warranted. For example, based upon a recommendation we received, we converted some of our documents into a PDF format to facilitate the ability to complete them online.

Obviously, we want financial gains but our greatest measure for success is twofold. I will first address what we call a great client. We track how we obtain our clients, candidates, and job orders. The referral sources allow us to evaluate where we are gaining new business. We find that a large number of candidate referrals are from individuals that we have met with, but have not necessarily been placed in a new position.

We also track our internal turnover. The executive search industry experiences high turnover and burn out. We continually look for ways to improve our environment for our employees so that we can minimize internal turnover. We provide flexible work arrangements, Web based technology to work at home, external training, and significantly more paid time off than industry standard.

The Future

The barriers to entry into the executive search industry are low. As a result, people who lack the training and appropriate level of professionalism can easily work in this field. Moreover, this lack of professionalism gives rise to the potential for unethical behavior. The result is that many people don't respect the services being provided by quality executive recruiting organizations. While this is not rampant, it is still significant enough that quality organizations spend an inordinate amount of time defending their industry and their fee structure. For me, this business is neither confusing nor difficult. You must remember that this is a people business. As recruiters, we facilitate the process but ultimately we do not have final control of the hiring decision. So we maintain our objectivity and we do not get emotionally involved in the outcome.

I not only lead my company but I also actively work my desk. Each day I not only do the things necessary to manage my business, such as negotiating contracts and managing employees, but I market the business to clients, call potential candidates, conduct interviews and reference checks among other things. I do not believe in competing with my consultants for placements. Fostering an environment of team work that is focused on making sure our client gets the best candidate for their position ensures that we do not get bogged down in a me versus we focus. Everyone celebrates in the success and rewards when we make a placement. I make myself available to coach and mentor but I also give my consultants the flexibility and the space to do their jobs. We have processes and procedures in place that we follow, but are not so stringent that it stifles an individual's creativity to be successful. I believe that my continued success after fifteen years in the business is attributable to my willingness to roll up my sleeves and work. Bottom line—I don't ask anyone to do anything I am not willing to do. More importantly, by actively working my desk, I am able to stay connected with what is really happening to my clients and candidates and stay in touch with the realities of the industry and marketplace.

We look for ways to incorporate technology that will allow us to be more efficient and free up our time to service our clients. I am a big supporter of training and education and promote certification in our business. My staff and I attend local and national training programs so we are always sharpening our skills. I am actively involved as a board member in our state and local industry associations, and network with my peers to continuously learn and implement improvements and best practices.

Advice to Other Executive Recruiters

Work your desk! You can make a great deal of money in this business but that should not be your primary goal. Remember to do the right things and keep your client's and candidate's best interests at heart. If you do this then the money will come. There is a reason for everything and if it is meant to happen it will. Remember it's a round world and what goes around comes around.

The largest misconception is that executive recruiters are not needed. Due to the evolution of technology and ability to access information, many companies feel they can just post a position on the job boards, or their Web site, and get all the candidates they need. They will get many candidates, but will they get appropriate candidates, and how much time do they have to sift through hundreds of applicants to find the most appropriate ones for the job? What this process lacks is the ability to utilize the extensive networks of the recruiting professionals to find the right person. At the end of the day, this is still a people business. The service we provide to our clients is valuable and greatly minimizes the time from the identification of a candidate to the hire. We know how to tap into the passive candidate market. The screening, interview, and selection process that we employ is a lot more sophisticated than simply posting a job description on one of the job boards. Because of the extensive interviewing and personnel assessments that we do, recruiters are in a much better position to assess the fit between a client and a candidate when it comes to determining the best client-candidate match.

I think a good customer relationship management (CRM) system is critical. It provides a central place to gather information about your clients and candidates, track communications, input job orders, and document all activity. On the candidate side it allows you to parse resumes and search the database for possible matches based on specific criteria you choose. A calendar, task and e-mail system allows everything to be at your fingertips. I have used Bullhorn for five years and this Web-based technology allows me to access my business information at any time and any place, resulting in much greater flexibility in my ability to do my job.

One of the biggest changes we are dealing with is access to information and instantaneous communication. When I entered this business we faxed resumes. I can't even imagine the days when everything was done by mail. Everything moves faster, and we expect it to move even faster as new technologies are employed. In addition, our business has gone from local to national. With the utilization of technology and good partnerships, we can now provide services to a much broader client base than we could in the past.

We have been hearing about the retiring baby boomers for a number of years, and the resulting shortage of talent that will exist for a number of jobs in the marketplace. We are already beginning to feel the crunch in the accounting and finance areas. Identifying quality talent, with fewer numbers of accounting students entering the profession, is also contributing to this crunch for talent. To address these issues, I believe that it will become socially and culturally acceptable for people in their seventies to hold key positions in companies. Companies will implement corporate wide retention strategies designed to keep their key talent. More individuals will be working from home or being provided the opportunity for flexible working arrangements. Companies will continue to look for ways to outsource their non-key business functions and strive to focus on their daily business operations.

As human capital becomes tighter, I see an increase in companies needing our assistance in the identification of the right talent. I see growth opportunities for companies that embrace a consultative approach for services that solve overall human resource problems such as developing retention strategies for organizations and performing skill set and competency reviews. Perhaps the three most important things for people in the executive research business to be doing at this time are the following:

Plan

I cannot emphasize enough how important planning is to being successful in this business. You need to plan, but more important, you need to work your plan. When I first entered the business I was told that you needed to do a little bit of everything every day. This can lead to a very disjointed and unproductive day if you take a haphazard approach to planning. The old-school method of planning had individuals putting everything down on paper. I believe individuals should utilize the best tools they have available to them. If you have a CRM system, then utilize the task and notes sections to plan your day. Be thorough and document relevant information that will save you time and effort later. I find that segmenting the day in one hour blocks dedicated to specific activities allows for the best focus and does not break your rhythm. Most important, find what works best for you and stick to it.

Know Your Clients and Candidates

There is no substitution for knowing everything you possibly can about your clients and candidates. Take a personal interest in their business and success and know that you must invest in them for them to be willing to invest in you.

Be Ethical

Be educated and conform to the accepted principles of right and wrong that govern our industry and strive for the highest standards of professional behavior. Follow the honorable course of action and do the right thing.

Lace Bourgeois Archibald, CTS, CSP, CERS, a former Deloitte & Touche LLP tax professional turned executive recruiter, partnered with Maxwell Locke & Ritter LLP in July of 1998 to spearhead the launch of ML&R Personnel Solutions LLC. Ms. Archibald earned her Bachelor of Science in business and public administration (marketing concentration) from The University of Texas at Dallas and her Masters in Accountancy from the University of Houston. Ms. Archibald's introduction into the staffing industry was with a small boutique-like staffing firm in Houston that provided accounting temporary services. An opportunity to start up and manage an international search firm brought her to Austin in 1996 and her entrepreneurial drive resulted in her decision to implement a lifelong goal and launch her own firm. Ms. Archibald is very active in her state and local staffing industry associations and participates in various community activities as well.

Dedication: *I would like to dedicate this chapter to the many clients, candidates, business associates, and internal team that allow me the opportunity to do what I love to do everyday—facilitate the placement of talented individuals in outstanding organizations. A special thank you is also extended to Mark Wey for allowing me to utilize him as a sounding board for my thoughts and ideas.*

Financial Industry Recruiting and Consulting Strategies

Michael Karp

Chief Executive Officer

Options Group

When I started my own executive search firm back in 1992 there were a lot of "headhunters" in this business, rather than people who were using an intelligent approach to the search process. At that time, Wall Street was looking to hire a number of experts in the business, finance, and mathematical fields; therefore, I decided to affiliate my firm with the top professionals at various universities, and we soon started getting referrals to all of the highly qualified Ph.D. students coming out of university math, physics, economics, and finance departments.

Today, our firm continues to base its success in the executive search field on having a better hold on the market in terms of intelligence and we use that intelligence to improve our effectiveness in the three services that we offer—executive search, market intelligence, and strategic consulting. We are primarily a retained search firm that recruits for financial services positions across the board, from technicians to CEOs.

Profit Growing Strategies: A Global Approach

In order to continue to grow profits successfully, our search firm has gone global; our ultimate goal is for our firm to be located in every financial money city in the world. We have gone into eleven different cities worldwide to date, and we are looking to open offices in some ten other cities as we search for great talent across far-flung regions.

Our profit growing strategies are also based on hiring young recruiters who view search as a long-term career, not simply a job where you make some money and then leave and go on to other things. Our offices across the globe are staffed by young, energetic, dedicated professional career search consultants.

Our global search focus is expanding because it is increasingly difficult to find the talent that our clients are looking for inside the U.S.—and everyone is looking for the same talent across the board. Indeed, many of the most talented people in the finance field are international students who have studied in the U.S. and now want to go back and work in their home countries. Therefore, we are seeing a lot of cross border hiring transactions, especially in emerging markets such as Eastern Europe, Moscow, Brazil, and China.

Creating an Effective Leadership Plan: A New Technology Focus

My leadership plan is aimed at turning our executive recruiting firm into a global executive consulting firm with a reputation for leadership not only in executive search, but also in the areas of market intelligence and strategic consulting. We want to see our firm go to the next level in the coming years and join the ranks of the top five recruiting/consulting firms, and in order to achieve that goal we need to be increasingly global and develop better technology.

To that end, we have created some unique tools to support our search and consulting practices. For example, we recently launched a system called Pachira, which tracks profit and loss (P&L) statements for hedge fund traders. Simply put, traders can log in their returns on our system, and we will maintain those returns on a monthly basis. Investors can consult our system to see which traders have performed consistently in terms of returning profits for their investors over a period of years.

A growing trend in the financial services recruiting field centers on the role of banks as recruitment process outsourcing houses. The more sophisticated the market becomes, the harder it is to find talent, and you need a firm such as ours to act as a middleman in terms of making key introductions. Professionals hate negotiating with their employers and Options Group can act as emissary on their behalf. Our firm, acting as search consultants, also can help candidates calculate their worth in the marketplace outside their present firm. (This is called market-to-market in the business). Our overall leadership plan is aimed at partnering with financial services firms in areas such as investment banking; global markets equity and debt; asset management; and hedge funds. We have about a hundred clients in the financial services field, and about 90 percent are retained, because we believe that a retained relationship is the best way to establish partnership and loyalty with your clients. Retained relationships allow an executive search firm the ability to provide not just recruiting, but market intelligence and consulting services as well. Real-time information is very important for banks and Options Group can provide it better with a retained relationship. .

Achieving Long-Term Success: Developing your Recruiters

In order to achieve long-term success as a search firm in this industry, you have to have a solid growth strategy, centered on the fact that your primary assets—your recruiters—walk in and out of your door on a daily basis. Therefore, you have to be competitive in terms of pay structures and the value that you bring to your recruiters. You have to be smarter than your competitors, and you must always strive to get your people engaged in bigger and better things. You must implement strategies to effectively grow your people across the board, and you have to run your business in such a way that your recruiters are an integral part of that business. Options Group sends all its search consultants each year to a "retreat" (this past year in Hawaii) to build up teamwork, brands, and strategy for the coming campaign.

In addition, each recruiter's role should be clearly focused. For example, if you are a hedge fund recruiter, you should be working for hedge funds, not banks, and if you are a bank recruiter specializing in credit derivatives, you should be focused exclusively on recruiting in credit derivatives and not on five different things. Generalist recruiters typically work for mom-and-pop shops, not global search firms.

Therefore, if you are aiming for long-term success in this field it is extremely important to ensure that all of your people are in sync. A team environment is something that needs to be promoted on a daily basis. Intelligence is also key—smart recruiters are more likely to succeed and stick with a firm.

Balancing Short- and Long-Term Goals

Short-term goals in this business are generally revenue-driven; for example, I am currently focused on developing other revenue-based products for our firm in the areas of market intelligence and strategic consulting. Our revenue goals are very aggressive, and we have achieved a consistent 15 percent growth rate over the last three years. We have put a very good management team in place; and we have created a very good management structure including a management committee that controls our domestic operations and an operating committee that runs our company on a global basis.

We have also built various high-tech systems that allow us to open an office for a client anywhere in the world within twenty-four hours, thanks to a very aggressive talent database. Indeed, I believe that such technology is essential in this field, because financial recruiting and consulting is becoming an increasingly intelligence-based business. Our financial services clients want to be able to know what their competitors look like at a click of a button; therefore, you have to invest a lot of time and effort into developing knowledge-based technology that serves the needs of this fast-growing field.

To that end, we recently opened a knowledge-processing center in India where we build all of our knowledge-based products. All of our research efforts take place at this center—name generating, profiling, market-to-market mapping, and composition analysis. We also have about 80 global consultants who keep us up to date on what is going on in their markets, and the global composition report in financial services that we produce as a result of their efforts is one of the leading across the board reports in this field.

Working with New Clients

When a client hires us, our primary goal is to establish a strong partnership with that client. First and foremost, we will meet with the client in order to evaluate how their company can benefit from our services. We will review all of their needs in relation to the search they are looking to conduct, and we will then quickly map their market and come back with a short list of candidates that are available. Within the next month we will interview those candidates, and then give the client a choice as to whether they want to proceed with an internal or external search—meaning whether the client wants to find candidates from inside his/her current firm or outside the firm. Our searches range from a very senior $5 million plus search to lower level searches.

We always evaluate the client company in order to determine how big their recruiting needs really are. For example, if a major bank needs to hire an investment banking professional, we will make a pitch for their entire analysts business, and if the client ultimately decides that they want to add fifty analysts, we will evaluate what the competition looks like, give them all of the necessary information with respect to their competitors' analysts, and let them pick and choose who they want to interview at the associate analyst level.

In many cases, we will come up with out-of-the-box ideas to meet the client's recruiting needs. If they are looking for pharmaceutical people, for example, to become analysts, we will go to pharmaceutical firms and try to find people who are highly educated and want to go into financial services. If they are looking for tech people, we will go to tech firms to find candidates. We have also done major programs and research for financial institutions that have asked us to create a diversity practice in the U.S., which is another way that we have separated ourselves from our competitors. For example, we recently completed a diversity research report for a global investment bank, breaking down its diversity levels and where it may need to increase diversity head count.

Meeting Challenges

We have often found that when you are recruiting for a senior level position in the financial services field, a candidate typically needs to be very motivated in order to make a move. In some cases, that motivation comes when someone else gets promoted over the candidate. In other cases, a candidate may be willing to change jobs if they feel that they have not been properly compensated at their present job, or if a competitor offers them a significant increase in salary or benefits. However, recruiting in this field is particularly challenging because in many cases, as soon as a candidate gets an offer from one of our clients, the institution that they are working for matches or counters that offer in some other way, simply because they do not want their senior officials to leave.

Another challenge of working in this industry is based on the fact that executive recruiting has become more of a talent management agent game than a headhunting game. I have worked with most of my clients and candidates for many years and they will deal only with me, even if some other search consultant calls them. Our view is that you have to act as an agent on behalf of both the client and the candidate, and that is not always an easy task. Indeed, it can be very difficult to succeed as an executive recruiter, because if you do wrong by anyone in this business word spreads very quickly—and reputation is a key factor in our business.

Profitable Strategies: Gaining Market Share and Building Customer Loyalty

Our search firm's main strategy for growing profits and gaining market share is to diversify our client base. Five years ago, for example, we did not have a huge hedge fund business; we concentrated solely on working for major banks. Today, we have close to sixty hedge fund clients on a global basis, and our hedge fund business has grown tremendously, as has our asset management and family office businesses.

Another strategy that we use to take market share away from other agencies is by selling clients our market intelligence services such as GAP analysis of businesses; organization charting and mapping; and compensation analysis. We also offer a strategic consulting service and a merger and acquisition (M&A) advisory business staffed by in-office expert search consultants that come from these backgrounds; they handle several of these very big "elephant hunt" structured deals each year. By elephant hunt, we mean that we sometimes will find teams of people to move from one firm to another. Of course, the most important strategy for gaining market share in this industry is to establish a long-standing relationship with our clients based on loyalty and trust. We always maintain a very strict "hands-off" policy, in that whenever a client retains us we utilize tight risk controls and compliance procedures on a global basis that stipulate where we can and cannot recruit. Our agreements in that respect are thoroughly screened; we have a "hands-off" committee that reviews every single contract that comes into the firm. Simply put, we never sign a contract with a client or candidate unless the management committee has signed off on it. Our clients need to be comfortable with our firm and know that if they retain us, they will not have to worry about us "poaching" people. Banks will not work with you if they can't trust you to abide by this rule.

Incorporating Market and Client Feedback

In order to ensure that we are providing quality client service at all times, we utilize the services of our internal marketing and content team, which constantly solicits client feedback with respect to our job performance. Each year we conduct a global offsite meeting in order to review market and client feedback; this year's meeting was attended by one hundred of our top consultants, who reviewed the feedback we received and then developed strategies for maintaining good client relationships going forward. Management teams are constantly changing and we want to make sure we are always tied in with the current team lineups so that we can cover all of our clients' recruiting needs from the top down, and give them the best possible service in the years to come.

If we find that we are not doing well in terms of a specific area of client search, we will try to repopulate our recruiting teams with people who have whatever expertise we do not currently possess. It is important to be up front with the client in that situation; we will tell them that we need more time to develop our expertise in a certain area, and therefore instead of finishing their search in one month, we may need three months to do the job.

Benchmarking

At the same time, we never sell the client any service that we cannot produce on, and our production rate has been consistently high. What really matters in this business is your ability to fill searches successfully, and over the last two years our firm has filled over 500 searches, a figure that represents a lot of hard work and strong execution.

In 2006, we put together a game plan for our company called "Mission 2009" and the goal of that mission is to achieve $100 million in revenues in financial services. We are now very close to achieving that goal. Our biggest fear has been attrition in our firm; therefore, at this year's offsite meeting our leadership team sat down with all the top people in our firm in order to explain where we are going, and what our long-term goals entail. We are working to eliminate a lot of the mom and pop shops; increase our global presence; penetrate those areas where our competitors are operating; and have their people join our team. Our technology is way ahead of our competitors, in terms of our global database, our P&L tracking system (Pachira) and our as yet unannounced E-commerce initiatives. We intend to keep this advantage by investing our money in R&D, so to speak, in the years to come.

Difficult Aspects of the Recruiting Business

One of the most difficult aspects of working in the recruiting business these days is dealing with the fact that there are too many headhunters on a global basis. When there is over liquidity in terms of agents who are trying to place people, many agencies will try cutting their fees by 5 to 15 percent—and it is difficult to pitch your services successfully when your competitors offer to do the same job for less. Therefore, it is important to promote the value of your across-the-board service offerings, especially when recruiting for senior level positions, whatever the industry focus. Marketing remains a very important aspect of this business, and branding is a key to the success of many companies because it is one way to differentiate your services from those of the competition.

Far too many recruiting firms are not relationship based; some do not even take the time to meet their clients, and/or run a recruiting business out of their houses, and that is not how I think this industry should be run—there should be a lot more professionalism across the board. Indeed, I believe that there should be a licensing process for search consultants involving courses on ethics in the recruiting business. Ethics in this business are very weak at the present time and may get worse as banks decrease their hiring patterns in 2008. But we are trying very hard to run our company as an ethical institution. It's never easy in a sales environment, but firms that lose the trust of their clients will be out of business by the end of this expected downturn. We plan on picking up that business by maintaining a certain level of trust with our clients. Other search firms will try and steal information as well as recruiters away and sometimes that can be unethical. We do not rely on getting information from other search firms.

Today's recruiting industry is a very fragmented industry, and it is getting increasingly difficult to consolidate it. The top five recruiting firms are basically loosely run franchises; they do not operate as a cohesive global firm—and it takes a lot of vision and collective power to create such a firm in such a tough and competitive industry.

The Importance of Innovative IP

In order to be truly innovative in this business, your firm needs to be technology driven. You should be able to show a client what their market looks like at a click of a button; and the only way to do that effectively is to use technology to effectively compile important data and Intellectual Property (IP).

Our firm's most valuable IP is our candidate database, which needs to be up to date and free of extraneous information. It is important to qualify all the candidates that go into our database so that we can always be sure that we are presenting our clients with the most highly qualified data. We keep our candidate database up to date through referrals; we keep track of people that our clients have wanted to recruit over the years; and we may even go to third party agencies to do background checks on a candidate's criminal and credit records to be sure that our database contains only quality candidates.

Industry Trends and Changes

Although there has been some consolidation in this industry in recent years, many mom-and-pop shops and small boutique recruiting firms have also sprung up, because once a recruiter is able to take their revenue to $5 million they often start to think that they can go into business on their own—although they soon find that it is not so easy to build a company successfully.

Many recruiting firms are focused on building a global team these days, and we are facing the same problems as our clients in terms of acquiring talent. We must also cope with a five-year cycle with respect to the time it takes to train someone who has come to our company from a securities firm until the time they are able to achieve effective results.

The biggest areas of growth for the recruiting industry in the years to come are likely to involve international, sector-based hedge funds which are able to raise the most assets. By running multi-strategy funds, these firms are able to attract institutional investors from all over the world. Regionally based funds in emerging markets that have posted consistently good returns will also raise substantial assets. All these funds don't have the infrastructure to recruit talent and will be particularly reliant on search firms like Options Group. Recruitment process outsourcing (RPO) is another growing trend in this business as banks attempt to automate parts of what can be a very lengthy recruiting process.

Helpful Advice

My advice to other leaders in the executive recruiting industry is to always pay your people competitively; take care of their needs; keep them constantly engaged in your business; keep challenging them; and keep showing them new and innovative ways of doing things. At the same time, you need to find ways to have fun and enjoy your work.

The only way to succeed in this industry over the long term is to work hard and stay constantly involved in the operations of your company. Indeed, my whole life revolves around this business.

Michael Karp is the embodiment of the American dream, leaving his middle-class family in New Delhi after high school to come to the United States. He met Options Group co-founder Bob Reed in college and started the firm initially known as Techno Placements in 1992 in New York. Fifteen years later, Options Group is the largest financial services-focused executive search firm in the world, with over 120 professionals in ten offices globally. Options Group, led by Mr. Karp's unwavering dedication, has doubled revenue since 2003 and is globally retained to execute searches by many of the top global investment banks and hedge funds.

The thirty-eight-year-old foresaw the growing importance of sales and trading on Wall Street in the 1990s and consequently spent over a decade networking with junior candidates around the world. These talented professionals now run many of the sales and trading desks that are seeking the next generation of employees. His intimate knowledge of these global markets has made him a popular media personality. Mr. Karp has been quoted in The Wall Street Journal, *the* New York Post, Crain's, *and regularly appears on* CNBC.

Mr. Karp also is a tireless supporter of Indian and Pakistani charities and backs a large number of organizations, including: Layton Rahmatulla Benevolent Trust (LRBT), which provides free eye care to Pakistanis; Developments in Literary, which promotes female literacy in Pakistan; Sakhi, a community-based organization committed to ending violence against women of South Asian origin; and Pratham, an Indian charitable organization that provides educational assistance in Mumbai. Crain's regularly lists Options Group as one of the top ten executive recruiters in the New York area.

Recruiting for Mission-Driven Organizations

John Isaacson

President

Isaacson, Miller

The Business

We handle senior level searches, typically involving the top three levels of the client organization. We charge one-third of the candidate's first year's cash compensation, as well as some of our expenses, which is standard practice in the retained search business. While there is some price competition in this industry, it is typically on the margin—the real competition in this business has to do with service and quality.

Among many other divisions, the retained search industry divides by size. There are about half a dozen firms that are genuinely global and large, with hundreds of millions of dollars in revenue. These firms are well known and compete in many different industry sections all across the globe. After the top six search firms there are a group of about fifteen firms that range in size from $4 to $35 million a year in revenues, and the rest of the industry is made up of firms consisting of two or three people billing between $300,000 and $4 million a year. Most of these small boutique firms have one narrow highly specific niche—i.e., recruiting bond traders for Wall Street, or independent school heads, or CIOs for hospitals. They are good, highly specialized businesses, with modest overheads. It is a good model. It is probably no accident that there are very few genuinely large global firms. Consolidation and scale work to build brand and to serve on a genuinely global scale. Similarly, it is probably no surprise that there are so few firms in the middle. It's always uncomfortable to be in the middle—not quite large enough to have the full economies of scale, but too large to be an efficient niche player.

A Unique Focus

Our search firm is in that middle category; we rank somewhere in the lower end of the top twenty search firms, and we have annual revenues of about $12 million a year. We define our marketplace as the mission-driven/civic institutions sector, and within that sector we work principally for not for profit organizations and a few government agencies, especially public universities. This is a bigger market sector than many people imagine; it probably accounts for 10 percent of the U.S. gross domestic product. We serve a series of well-defined fields within the sector—higher education; scientific institutions; foundations; K-12 schools; health care organizations;

arts and culture organizations; fundraising/development; advocacy, especially in the area of human and civil rights; environmental defense; community based social services; and community based economic development. Some of the specialty territories within the mission-driven sector, such as higher education and health care, are themselves large, both as a field and as a practice, and each contains many sub-niches within the field.

We have a great many competitors, large and small, but they're usually focused on one field or one sub-niche within the field. We have very few firms that focus on the sector and no one else of our size operates sector wide. We recruit our staff from people with fundamental mission commitments. Many of them made an early commitment to one of our key fields. They have often pursued graduate studies in a relevant field. We are a group of people committed to the work of public civic missions. When we get a new search, we are excited by making the sale, but we are most excited by what our clients do. Simply stated, we are inspired by our clients. They do remarkable work.

Profit-Growing Strategies

We believe that "production drives sales." If we do really first-rate work for our clients, they will appreciate our efforts, and they will send more work in our direction. We do not know when or how that work will come—it may be in the form of a referral, peer to peer, to a completely different organization, even across fields, or it may be repeat business for the same client, but we believe that if we do first-rate work, we will grow.

This underlying philosophy has considerable implications for how we staff our organization; our division of labor practices; the culture we try to build; and the attitude we have toward our work. As a mission-driven business serving mission-driven organizations, we hire people who have drunk the Kool-Aid—only highly motivated people join and stay with our organization.

Second, we believe that every piece of work that we do is a fundamental marketing tool. That belief has motivated us to hire staff members who are willing to work more intensively on the nature of their craft and to invest in our culture of service. If our people are optimizing the last dollar and cutting corners, it doesn't work in our culture. Over the course of twenty-five years in this business we have gotten better organized, better staffed, more structured, and more knowledgeable about what constitutes good search work, and we have retained a lot of people with highly developed consciences, who are inclined to overdo their work.

Balancing Short- and Long-Term Goals

We have two core goals for the next few years—to grow and to become the "essential" quality firm in the markets that we believe are central to our mission and our economics.

We believe that we will ultimately become a stronger and more resilient company in the years to come if we are able to grow somewhat larger than we are now. We do not intend to become a genuinely large firm. We seek a size where we can have a leadership impact in our key fields, without constantly running into conflicts of interest, where we can build strong and efficient overhead functions with good economies of scale and we seek to remain a very personal community.

Size helps. We have improved our quality by adding central overhead functions, a good finance staff, complex databases, a research function, marketing, professional development, centralized recruiting, all of which scale well. As we grow, we are able to retain earnings and gain economies of scale. Fortunately, we have been able to consistently grow at an average rate of 10 percent a year, and we want to continue to achieve that rate of growth for at least the next few years.

On the mission side, we want to become the "essential" or "go-to" or "must-have" firm in our chosen fields. While we are already a contender in each of those fields, we want to be the essential firm—the one people feel they must come to if they want to get the best work. We know there is hubris in that goal and that you are only as good as the work you do. We know that is a difficult goal to achieve, but we are clear. That is the brand we seek. Growth is essential to achieving this goal. We believe that if we were somewhat larger than we are now we would be able to generate the type of revenues that would allow for a stronger staff development and training function, and more highly developed systems. It takes dedicated professional staff who work hard on craft development, on training, and on systems to build consistent quality. Growth has strengthened us.

The firm was built on its mission. We are inspired when we can see over the years that we have made a contribution; when we can see that our clients are well led, have strengthened their organizations, and are doing good work in the world. We want the opportunity to serve some of the most important institutions in our fields; they can be small or large, prominent or unknown. We don't discriminate by pedigree. We want to serve the organizations whose ambitions are large, whose missions are critical, and whose people are coherent.

We believe that if we execute on our mission and grow steadily to a more optimum size we will also become a more profitable, higher quality, and more resilient firm.

Managing a Search: A University Example

Half of our work is for colleges and universities. We use the same methods in that market that we do in all our others, but it's easier for me to illustrate what we do because for the last few years I have focused much of my attention on colleges and universities. University presidencies are a modest part of our higher ed business but they illustrate the case. They attract a lot of attention and a rigorous process is rewarded. We launch by meeting with the university's search committee and organizing a timetable for the search. A rigorous timetable is critical to success. Searches are full of people and they all have their own agendas. If the client and the firm anchor their efforts in a rigorous schedule, we are far less likely to be distracted and far more likely to succeed. We then organize what we call a "scoping process." Over the course of two days (or more) we meet with the search committee, then the client's senior officers, the outgoing president if possible, the provost, the vice presidents, the deans, the faculty, department chairs, and some open meetings at all of the key levels of the organization. We will visit the university's medical center, if they have one, and spend time with all of its senior officers as well. We will then have at least one long meeting with the search committee about the future they envision for the university. At all of these meetings we will ask a fairly simple question: After you hire your next president, how will you know that he or she succeeded?

We have an analytic frame that helps us approach that question. We think about mission-driven organizations as containing three leadership dimensions: mission, market, and management. Success inevitably means aligning all three parts and scoping is an effort to see where the client came from, how they are now positioned, and where they are going. We are grubbing around, looking for the unsaid, for the "theory in action," the ideas that actually motivate a place, not the ones that are necessarily written down.

1. What are the underlying values that are driving this organization; what identity and mission do they say they have in the academic world, do they say they want in the academic world? Do they behave in ways that are consistent with a clear mission or does their behavior reveal an alternative mission?

2. What market does the organization serve? What is sustaining this enterprise? Does it have enough students? Are they paying full tuition, or is the tuition discounted? Are its graduate schools highly ranked? Do they attract who they want as both faculty and Ph.D. students? Do they attract full pay masters students to professional schools? What level of sponsored research is coming from the government? What is the indirect cost return rate allowed by federal agencies and is that adequate? What's the endowment? What is the nature of alumni support? Is the development effort sophisticated? Is there a medical center, and what is its position in the clinical marketplace? Does it offer medical care at a significant discount? Does it carry a free care burden? Is its hospital achieving net revenues sufficient for new capital investment? Are there transfers going to the academic side from the clinical side in order to support the institution's academic mission? These are all relevant market questions.

3. Finally, does this institution deliver the kind of academic product, service to students, and quality of research that is consistent with either its explicit or implicit mission. Do they know where they stand? Do they recruit vigorously for students and faculty? Do they use their money carefully and maximize? Are they organized to plan, to allocate? Are they inventive where they are weak?

We think of leadership as making the three parts work together. Leaders get people excited about the core values. They get scientists to stay all night in the lab and believe that what they do will make a fundamental difference. They celebrate the pathbreaking controversial new scholarly work that faculty do, because the ideas of the next generation count. They attend to student life because they want to see young people grow. Then they find the money. They sell a clear mission. They marry mission to market. They say, accurately, "We care about undergraduate education and we particularly cater to first generation students. We have a cooperative work program that links learning to work, making a student's education meaningful and powerful." That underlying mission will attract donors, students, families, and corporate sponsors. It has a clear defined meaning and it has a market. Leaders define things and they sell them. I often describe this as the ability to marry virtue to wealth, mission to market.

Leaders, we are famously told, don't manage things. I suspect that is not quite true. A leader who couldn't manage his/her own staff, who couldn't create a dependable set of expectations for an organization, wouldn't be much of a leader. It is true that leaders stay up out of the weeds and make sure "the right things" happen, but good management is one of the things that has to happen. A badly managed, mission-driven organization that can't deliver on its vision is an organization that will fail. If the president does a lovely job of defining a great undergraduate focused university, with an emphasis on first generation students, and raises money, but the faculty and students experience their daily lives as a set of empty rhetoric, then the house of cards will eventually collapse. Real leadership is made up of all three parts and real leaders make sure all three parts are aligned.

Scoping is an effort to understand. We don't have much time—a few days on campus. We get to see a lot of very smart people and if we can focus enough, ask enough questions and remember what we have been told, we will get a little smarter. The test comes when we try to write it down. We write a scope that runs somewhere from five to twenty pages that describes the context for the university (or any other client): its history and mission, the sources of its revenue and their trend lines, and the management successes it has had in the past that affect its present position.

At the core of the document, we draft for the client a section of "challenges and opportunities." In broad strokes, it describes what the new leader has to do to live up to the client's aspirations. We will generally make a list of not more than five to six challenges—a much longer list is a laundry list. In the last section, we list the qualifications that a candidate would need to have to succeed with these challenges. In drafting the document, we are relying entirely on the client's reporting and on their clearly articulated ambitions. Scopes typically go through a few drafts and we work closely with the search committee in order to make sure that we have come to the right conclusions. The committee drives the process. We are staff, hard working staff to be sure, but just staff. We have to get it right and we have to get it right in their terms. That's the test of an intense couple of weeks. Did we hear accurately? Did we understand what we heard? Did we say it in a way that does credit to our client? Does it pose the right challenges for the future? When the search committee owns the scope, and believes in it, then we are ready to go to market and recruit.

Finding the Right Candidates

The hunt always begins with the core business of the organization. Imagine, for a moment, recruiting the vice president for global warming at an environmental foundation. The global climate program has a real mission—to alter the way the U.S. understands the global climate threat. The foundation has focused on economic incentives to reduce the emission of climate changing gases. It makes grants to advocacy groups and research institutes. It seeks a new leader who can make the esoteric meaningful in the public policy arena.

This is a knowable universe. We are looking for candidates with a lot of experience with carbon emissions and climate change; who understand the fundamental economics of how regulatory systems work, and are able to make a persuasive argument for those systems in the political arena. Mostly we are looking for someone with good judgment about people. We would start with a list of all of the most influential and knowledgeable people in the global climate world. The database is our first stop and it has a few hundred relevant names. We have done work in the field before. If we have a particular angle of vision we want to pursue, we could turn to our research office and ask them to help us figure out who are all the key organizations that fund research, do research or advocate in the global climate debate. These are source and prospect lists. Sometimes we know them. Sometimes we don't. And we never know how it will come out. We launch, sending e-mails and making calls. Success comes when we stir people up, when we find people who are excited by the story we are telling, in print and in person, and who begin to make us smart about other people. It is an instant learning exercise about a field, conducted on the phone. It's personal, gossip filled, and intense. We are conducting a systematic sweep of a plausible universe. We will ask advice of the best people in the field. We triangulate their advice and we woo candidates. It is labor intensive painstaking work, but eventually, we discover the right people and persuade some of them to join the search. Strong searches have deep pools with many good choices. They are hard to do.

The Interview Process and Reference Checking

In the last phase of a search, we shift gears, from defining and finding to knowing. We have early clues. Our sources on the network have opinions and we encourage them to tell us confidentially what they think. This is high quality gossip, evidence of a sort, but not dispositive—a useful set of clues. It guides us towards the right people and it informs our first interviews. We have hypotheses to test.

We schedule phone interviews and then face-to-face interviews, either by video or in person. We are interested in the professional biographies of our candidates. We track their careers, one step at a time, looking for the progression, seeing what they choose and what they avoid, and shopping for the evidence of success. An interview takes a couple of hours, sometimes more. We are looking for prior work and evidence of prior success at tasks that are at least vaguely comparable to the challenges in front of this foundation. We want to know how the candidate chose an early career—what drew them to the environmental field; what brought them into the global climate world; how grounded they are in the applicable science; what they have learned about the economics of the field; how involved they have been in the politics of the field; how persuasive and influential they are; what judgment they use in order to determine which projects to back; and whether any of their past victories and successes are similar to what this foundation might need them to do. Interviews are useful. You can see the core pattern of personal choice. You can formulate a good hypothesis about character and some of the fact pattern around the work comes clear. It is not, however, history. It is autobiography, a narrative composed by an interested narrator. It has a genuine relationship to history, but it is not history.

Our clients make judgments at this stage. We have the results of two interviews, one on the phone, one in person, and some useful high level gossip, in the form of preliminary references acquired during the networking (the finding.) We present our discoveries to the client. They see it all. They see all the lists and all the people. They hear reports from us on our interviews and early references. They also know people, have their own impressions, and have probably done some informal references. We are not shy. We make recommendations about who we believe they should interview, but the choice is fundamentally theirs. They usually interview somewhere between five to ten people, depending a great deal on the field and the role. The committee usually interviews as a group over a couple of days. The process can vary, depending on the committee's size and the organizations' culture. In a first round of client interviews, the committee will usually narrow the field to three or four top candidates. Then we begin intensive reference checks, sometimes aided by committee members, if they have key relationships. The references are "up, down and sideways, on and off the list,"—that is bosses, peers, and subordinates—and names that the candidates want us to call, and names that they have not given us. Each reference check call will typically take about thirty to forty-five minutes; we usually check some six to fifteen references per finalist. There are no guarantees. The world of leadership implies turmoil and risk. What we do, aiding our clients to find leaders, is inherently risky, but we can reduce risk and increase the probability of success. We rely on history. We learn from the candidate and we learn from all the critical observers who surround the candidate. We bring the results to the client and they choose. We think of our disciplined, historical learning as a core competitive advantage and a central part of our culture

Gaining Market Share

We are a labor intensive firm. We are building brand through quality. In search anything that you can imagine going wrong will eventually go wrong. It is full of people and they all have a will of their own. We grow when we do our job right and are referred for new business. We have been aided in our efforts by some degree of specialization. Our quality clearly improved when we added a strong associate cadre to our staff. The specialized reference checkers got trained. We did more references than we did before and they were better. We organized by teams and recruited administrative staff for the teams. They made us more organized, more responsive. The research and database functions made the teams better. The constant attention to craft made us all a little smarter

We probably spend more money on our searches than our competitors. We have made a deliberate investment in a high end service. It has its costs, but we do it knowingly, taking a little less home. It is a strategy with some dangers, but it has worked. We have chosen mission-driven fields. We recruit mission-driven people and we try to infuse the work with a quality mission. It has been a consistent long-term strategy and it has given us a growing brand and a constantly improved market position.

Client Service: Building Customer Loyalty

We often describe ourselves as a craft intensive company, meaning that every meeting that we have will include some discussion about some point of craft—i.e., some aspect of how we have been doing our searches. We believe that professional development is not a separate special area—it is a major part of what goes on at our firm on a daily basis, and we want to do more of it.

Over the long run, we will need more investment in craft. We have an apprentice culture, though we have moved, as resources permit, to a knowledge management culture, with more formal writing, teaching, and learning. The best business talk that we have is craft talk. It is what engages the staff. They learn by doing. They learn from each other and they want to share the insight. Slowly we have built a craft culture, with a shared view of best practice. It's an evolving effort. It has taken us years to build a body of knowledge and to convey it broadly. In the long run, it will be the strongest of our assets.

Incorporating Market and Client Feedback

We conduct surveys at the end of each of our searches. We usually know how we have done, but this is a useful, more formal check. We ask a full range of performance-related questions—i.e., did we understand the client's business? Did we deliver good candidates? Was our timing satisfactory? Over time, as we develop resources, I suspect we will track our candidates and their success more closely. We would learn something if we did surveys one year and three years and five years out. It is labor intensive and for the moment we choose to invest in the searches themselves, but over time we could move that way.

We are not a big enough firm to do real marketing surveys; that would measure the strength of our brand, especially by our sub fields, but we track our repeat and referral business, and that rate has moved up over the years. Sixty-six percent of our searches are repeat work from a prior client, and our referral rate is substantial as well, though we don't track it as assiduously.

Difficult Aspects of the Executive Search Business

Any people-based business has inherent difficulties. We have our own teams and our own people to train and manage. At leadership transition time, the conflicts emerge within our client's organization. The sources we rely on in our networking have highly disparate points of view and our candidates are usefully idiosyncratic. As the search develops, we learn things we didn't want to learn. The candidates get excited or deflated. The candidate's families, spouses, and children weigh in on disruptive moves. Existing employers counter offer. Reference checks sometimes tell you the truth and sometimes don't. It's a people business. It's inherently complicated.

We succeed by organizing against the risk. We need to accurately understand our client. We need to accurately explain it to the relevant world. We need to explain our client's goals to our candidates in a coherent way and to discover whether those candidates are genuinely prepared for the role that you are describing. Executive recruiting is a long, careful effort to do something rational in a territory of highly dissident voices.

The Importance of Innovation

We succeed if we remain a learning organization. We learn in our craft and we learn in our fields if we challenge our own conventional wisdom. If we are constantly learning new craft, we stay alive. If we are exposed to the best minds in our fields and we attend carefully to what they say, we begin to know what it takes to do these jobs right. We are better when we are constantly learning. My first search was for a commissioner of corrections; I stumbled for a while and then I started asking, "What would constitute a good prison?" I found people who would engage with that question and who had credible answers. It is what built the right network. I started the business, with a search from my original mentor, for a director of aviation. I learned that running airports is not about flying planes, it is about moving people. It is ground transportation. Eventually that defined the network.

I once read that the main difference between a very good school and a very bad school is the difference between who is learning and who is not. If the students are the only ones who are expected to learn and the teachers are not, then the school will soon become dull. The teachers will be doing all the talking, and the students will be doing all the listening and eventually both sides will get bored. However, if everybody in the school is in constant learning mode, it will be an exciting place, a risky place, because no one knows exactly how it will come out, but an exciting place, where real learning will actually occur. That is probably true of a search firm as well; if we are constantly learning new things about the substantive areas that we work in, as well as the craft of search, then we will be an exciting company, and we will succeed.

The Future of Search

The executive/retained search industry is relatively new; this is not an industry with very deep roots. In its early days, most recruiters were essentially telemarketers who gave the industry a rather seedy reputation;

many individuals viewed recruiters as people who stole loyal employees away from their otherwise happy careers.

Today, the executive search industry has become increasingly global and broadly accepted. Most people realize that recruiters can perform a valuable function in today's competitive workplace. They maximize inefficient labor markets, moving highly skilled executives to organizations where they are more usefully employed.

The executive search industry is a straightforward example of how the modern workplace embraces competition and how organizations adapt. Something is gained and something is lost. The business has grown rapidly on the corporate side, but it has grown much more slowly on the mission-driven side; partly because there is less money in that area, but also because these tend to be more stable, enduring, long-term organizations. As the mission-driven fields become more competitive, and as leaders move more often, they have turned increasingly to search. Executive search has been a fast-growing field in recent times, and we have been fortunate enough to be in the field, and to grow with it. I see the field continuing to grow. It will reflect the pace of the economy and the shape of each industry's own growth. New technologies will affect it, though it is so personal that I suspect the technology will always operate on the margin. It has gone global. It is not yet clear if that will be as true for mission-driven organizations as it has been for business. Most civic organizations still recruit most of their leadership within their national boundaries. It has been a terrific if sometimes terrifying ride. I doubt that will change.

John Isaacson founded Isaacson, Miller in 1982. He is a graduate of Dartmouth College, Oxford University, and Harvard Law School. Following law school, he chose a career in public service. He served three gubernatorial administrations as an appointed official, where among other duties he was responsible for executive search. At Isaacson, Miller he has participated in search across the full range of public missions. In more recent years, he has taken particular responsibility in academic medical and higher education search, leading many of the firm's academic leadership searches.

Taking a Targeted Approach to Executive Searches

Rick Gillham

President

Gillham, Golbeck and Associates Inc.

The Recruitment Process

As an executive recruiting firm, we face a unique challenge: we are typically hired by client companies to fill executive leadership positions with the type of individuals who are not actively looking for a job. In order to attract those candidates, we must first confer with our clients to come up with an effective job presentation which includes a description of the client company, as well as a specific job description. Our Research Department then will produce a list of the company's main competitors and the individuals within those companies who might hold a position similar to the one that the client wants to fill.

A Targeted Approach

Indeed, we always take a highly targeted approach to the recruiting process by developing a call list which enables us to go after only those people who meet the client's specific requirements. In many cases, the candidates whom we interview have been referred to us by other clients or by candidates with whom we have worked in the past. We typically have some frame of reference about each of the candidates that we place, and we rarely make cold calls to find candidates.

Once we have found a number of promising candidates, we take them through a fairly lengthy interviewing and reference checking process in order to determine if they are a match for our client. Next, we discuss with our client the best two or three candidates that we have interviewed and set up client interviews with those candidates. Our ultimate goal is to ensure that at the end of the recruiting process we have a candidate who is as interested in our client company as the company is in our candidate. We want to be sure that if an offer is made, it is likely to be accepted.

In order to save time and trouble for our clients, we manage and schedule the entire interview process. Although we do not do any candidate testing ourselves, we administer tests our clients may provide. We then manage the offer process and guarantee the candidates that we place for a six-month period. In order to live up to that guarantee, we keep close tabs on our candidates during that six-month period in order to make sure that everything is going well.

Analyzing the Client's Culture

The success of our recruiting process is based, in part, on the fact that we spend a significant amount of time making sure that our candidates fit in with our client's corporate culture. This fit is often as important as making sure that they match the criteria of the client's job description. Even if the work is satisfying, an employee will not stay long if he or she does not enjoy being on the team.

Some of our clients have very well-defined corporate cultures, such as The Staubach Company. This group has been recognized as a top employer by its high employee satisfaction rating. However, some newer companies do not have an established culture, and for those clients we have developed a three-page document to help our clients define, or at least identify, elements of their culture. This is used as part of our job presentation and criteria-defining process. The culture-defining document asks questions such as: "What are three reasons someone would want to leave where they are and come to work at this company?" Other questions include: "What is unique about your organization? What is your management philosophy? What is said about your company in the marketplace?"

Profit-Making Growth Strategies

We base our company's success on the fact that we do not dilute our recruiting process. For the most part, the person that goes out to sell our business to potential clients is also the same person that will execute on the client's search. If I am the individual who visits with the client and helps them to put together a good job presentation, then I am likely to be the most qualified person to give that presentation to a potential recruit. It does not make sense to hand that job off to someone else at the firm.

Our recruiters believe in being very hands on with all of our clients. Although we do have some help internally—i.e., our research department helps us find potential candidates—for the most part our individual recruiters remain the key touch-point with respect to our clients and candidates. We are committed to returning every phone call from clients and candidates alike and showing common courtesy to everyone. Although our clients pay us and they are officially our "customer," we try to show the candidates on the other side of the recruiting equation an equal amount of respect. This helps to keep our network of industry contracts active. In many cases, our candidates later become our clients.

An Effective Leadership Plan

Our company's vision is focused on recruiting for the commercial real estate industry, which has become more of a global enterprise in recent years. Therefore, my plan to expand and effectively lead this recruiting group is based on diversifying our company geographically. To that end, we recently hired a team member who will build our business in the northeast and the Mid-Atlantic regions—areas on which we have not previously concentrated. We also have experts on staff who focus on recruiting for tropical resort environments and specific metropolitan areas.

Not only are we looking to expand geographically, but also in terms of property type. We have largely focused on recruiting for office, industrial, retail, and multi-family real estate companies. We also make many financial placements in the real estate industry. However, in the past few years we have seen growth in the areas of student housing, military housing, resorts, and medical facilities as well.

Because our primary focus is on commercial real estate recruiting, we have not seen the same slowdowns that the residential side of the business has seen. While some of our debt-related clients have put the brakes on searches because of the current credit crunch, we have not seen the major drop-offs that others have seen on the residential side of the industry.

Matching Clients and Candidates

The real estate industry is a fairly small community, and we are familiar with most commercial real estate companies. However, before going into the recruiting process it is essential to meet with a potential client face-to-face. We like to talk to the people that the candidate will be working for and working with, so that we can get a sense of what their working environment will be like. Much of this evaluation process is also intuitive; the longer you work in the recruiting industry, the easier it is to determine who is going to fit into a given company's culture. Recruiters often develop a sixth sense regarding these matters.

At the same time, we try to spend as much time with our candidates as possible in order to determine what type of working environment they are looking for. It is a two-way street: we have to make sure that the environment that our candidates prefer matches with what our clients are offering. It can be more difficult to make that assessment when we do a long distance search. In those cases, we may have to spend more time on the phone with the potential candidate, and if we are doing a search for an out-of-town client, we may need to fly out to meet with them. We rarely do a search for a client or a candidate we have not met face-to-face.

Reference Checking Procedures

Although personal impressions are important, reference checking is another crucial step in the recruiting process. We obtain the names of references directly from the candidate, and we use a special ten question form while interviewing these references to ensure that the same things are addressed with each person. Typically, we check three to five references on each candidate. In many cases, we have been referred to our candidates by someone we already know and have worked with in the past; therefore, we usually know something about the candidate going into the recruiting process. However, once we have determined that the candidate is interested in a particular job, and that our client has a mutual interest in the candidate, we do check the candidate's references. Questions will inevitably arise during the interviewing process that we like to incorporate into our reference-checking process—i.e., what were the candidate's greatest strengths in a previous position or how would you characterize their leadership skills?

Top Recruiting Challenges

We are currently experiencing an employee-driven market: there are many more jobs than people qualified to fill them. The competition for candidates is fierce, and people who have any experience at all in this industry are typically called by more than one recruiter. Therefore, our biggest challenge is finding ways to differentiate our client's job opportunity from all the others that are available. When we call potential candidates and tell them that we have been retained by a certain company to conduct a search on their behalf, that generally connotes that the company is approaching their job search in a serious manner. But that is not enough. The recruiter needs to determine what can be said to potential candidates about our client's company and the position being offered that is going to attract them. We must really work with the candidate to establish what is unique and fulfilling about the opportunity. Taking this approach to the recruiting process is essential. The unemployment rate is falling because fewer people are coming into the marketplace and others are retiring in record numbers. Finding qualified candidates will continue to be a major issue for the recruiting industry for many years to come.

The Financial Impact of Successful Recruiting

The biggest financial impact that we make on our client companies is based on the fact that we can find candidates that our clients would typically be unable to locate on their own. Our recruiters' unique combination of eighty years in the recruiting industry and the skill of experts in our Research Department enable us to provide the best qualified candidates to our clients.

Our expertise in terms of identifying our clients' culture and environment, and our ability to analyze and understand the workplace quality of life issues that are so important to today's younger workers, also helps us find people who will want to stay with our client companies. It is hard to put a price tag on the value of that process. However, if you consider that it typically costs more than twice someone's annual salary to replace them, there is a direct economic benefit to using our service. In addition, we guarantee every candidate that we place for a period of six months. Simply put, it is more cost effective to pay our fee and find the right person for the job than it is to replace an unsuccessful candidate.

Gaining Market Share

Our company's ability to gain market share from our competition is based primarily on our hands-on approach to the recruiting process. Our company is somewhat unique in that each recruiter is the contact person for their particular client in every aspect of the search process.

Our ability to gain market share is also due to the face that we focus on just one area—commercial real estate—and we are collectively networking through fourteen different real estate organizations. In some cases our involvement consists of board and committee-level positions within these groups. Our national network is huge, and we are also becoming known as an international search firm. Important as well is our proprietary database containing 32,000 individuals from which we can draw referrals.

Our success is also based on the fact that each of our recruiters has different skill sets. For example, my partner is a CPA, and she places a lot of accounting and finance people in real estate. One of our other recruiters has spent twenty years in asset and property management. Another colleague handles all of our resort and financial services recruiting, and two others have fourteen years of collective experience in the construction and development areas of the industry. We draw on all of these areas of expertise in order to gain market share in our field.

The Importance of Client Service and Feedback

Our ability to generate revenues is also based on the fact that we always focus on our client's goals. Although we have a successful recruiting process in place, we can be flexible in meeting specific needs. Indeed, we encourage input from our clients during the search process, because we view this process as a partnership arrangement, rather than as a vendor relationship.

We strive to find candidates that are going to add value and revenue to the client's company and help them to grow their business. We are not interested in doing one-off searches. Once we understand a client company's culture and needs, we want to continue working for that company on other searches. Some 85 percent of our searches are for repeat clients. Over the years, we have done close to one hundred searches for specific clients, thus becoming more of a recruiting extension of our client's business than an outside vendor.

In most cases, we communicate with our clients at least once a week in order to let them know how their search is progressing. We also like to get feedback from our clients at the end of the search with respect to what they liked about what we did, and what would they change, because we want to get consistently better at what we do. Of course, we really have two customers—the candidate and the client. We need to make them both happy, because our referral network of candidates and clients is our main asset. Thus, we will ask our candidates the same questions with respect to their views of our performance during the search process. Our recruiters also have internal discussions about what went right and wrong during our searches and what we could have done better, so that we can learn from one another.

Benchmarking Strategies

We have an annual billing goal, an annual placement goal, and an annual send-out goal, which are the measures of what we do. We know how many people we have to send out on interviews to make a placement; we know how many placements we have to make in order to reach our billing goal; and we know what our average fee is. We can actually analyze this data to determine the number of calls that we need to make to fill a particular position.

Difficult Aspects of the Executive Recruiting Business

Perhaps the most difficult aspect of working in the executive recruiting industry is dealing with the negative perception that many clients and candidates have about the recruiting process, due to negative experiences they have had with other search firms. Although that negative perception is not as prevalent as it used to be, we must always strive to educate our clients about how we handle the search process. Many clients think that when they give us a job we just go back to our desk, reach into a drawer, pull out five resumes, send them over to the client, and then hope that they hire one of those candidates. Of course the search process is a lot more involved than that.

Difficulties can also arise on the candidate's side of the recruiting equation. Candidates often call us after they have been laid off or when they are looking to change jobs. We like to know about this, even if we are not working on a search that we think would be a good fit for their needs. They need to be in our referral network and an appropriate position could surface at any time. We do not, however, offer to find them a job; that is not the business that we are in. As a retained search firm, we are in the business of filling jobs that we are hired to fill—we do not market candidates.

Executive recruiting can also be a very difficult business because there is no science to what we do. There are a lot of moving parts. Successful recruiting is largely an abstract process based on identifying the essence of your client's needs and working environment, and finding the candidate who best matches those requirements. Keeping the parties who are involved in the recruiting process encouraged and motivated when things are not going well can be very challenging. We do our best to communicate frequently with our candidates. Keeping them updated on the search process is a good way to reduce anxiety.

It can also be challenging to deal successfully with the many different kinds of personalities who typically work at an executive search firm. It can even be difficult to determine which recruiters will fit in best with your own corporate culture. There are no easy answers because no one personality type makes a better recruiter than another, and it takes all kinds of people to succeed in this business.

The Importance of Innovation

Innovation and differentiation are essential to success in this field. Our executive recruiting firm, for example, has focused on being a part of the real estate industry and on making this a very high-touch, one-on-one operation. In terms of technology, we have created a very sophisticated, Web-based database with significant search and reporting capabilities. By continually updating this proprietary information, we have tried to stay on the cutting edge of what is happening in the industry.

However, I believe that innovative technology is not as important as finding good recruiters who really care about the clients and candidates; indeed, the quality of our recruiters is more important to our company than being the biggest recruiting firm, having the most extensive geographic reach, or billing the most clients.

Recent Trends and Upcoming Growth Areas

I believe that the search business is still in its infancy in many respects. Twenty-five years ago a candidate who was looking for a job would often pay their own fee, a practice that is unheard of these days. At that time employment agencies would typically receive resumes and then try and match them up with their clients. Agencies were primarily in the business of marketing candidates. They rarely spent time developing a client's job presentation and description, or analyzing their corporate culture.

Today's recruiting industry is much more consultative than it used to be. We work as partners with our clients in the search process, and I believe that trend will become even more prevalent in the coming years. In addition, I believe that recruiters will be expected to provide many ancillary services outside of the search process in the years to come—i.e., skills training, compensation input, surveying and strategic planning as it relates to hiring.

It is likely that our client base will not be as large in the coming years, simply because of the talent shortage. Further, if we place someone in a company, we do not recruit candidates from that client company. To succeed in the future, we must establish many long-term partnerships with clients who view us as their search provider and counselor for employment-related services.

Helpful Advice and Golden Rules

If you want to succeed as an executive recruiter, you need to remember that you are dealing both with a company's success and people's livelihoods. You are dealing with human beings on both sides of the recruiting process who have needs and expectations. I believe that everybody—clients and candidates alike—should be treated fairly and with respect. Therefore, my three golden rules for success in the executive search business are simply this: always treat others with courtesy; always practice ethical behavior; and always do unto others as you would have them do unto you.

During the years since Rick Gillham founded the firm in 1982, Gillham, Golbeck & Associates, Inc. has become one of the most respected real estate executive search firms in North America. He has led his team of consultants in completing challenging assignments for many top real estate companies across the United States and internationally. Mr. Gillham emphasizes the firm's advisory role in partnering with clients to investigate and evaluate their needs, assets, liabilities, and growth potential. By analyzing each situation's unique requirements, his firm brings clients an understanding of the best ways to attain the skills, talents, and resources needed to realize their goals.

Mr. Gillham is a graduate of the University of Texas, El Paso. His professional experience encompasses sales, marketing and human resources for both national and global companies, and he is a member of TREC (The Real Estate Council), ULI (Urban Land Institute), IREM (Institute of Real Estate Management), ICSC (International council of Shopping Centers), and NTCAR (North Texas Commercial Association of Realtors).

Building a Transparent Recruiting Process

Alex E. Preston
President
The Energists Ltd.

The strategies that I first developed when I created this search firm twenty-eight years ago have helped us to become worldwide specialists in the energy sector of the recruiting industry. One key strategy that enables our firm to stand strong is our focus on hiring high integrity professionals with previous experience in the energy field. There is a great deal of turnover in the executive search business. However, unlike most search firms that have a revolving door, we have developed the ability to retain our recruiters for the long-term, because we hire the best people and pay them the best rates in the industry.

Reinventing the wheel in terms of recruiting strategies is not needed, but I do insist greatly on seamlessness and transparency in the recruiting process. To that end, it is incredibly important to be meticulous about the recruiters that are brought into the firm. Our consultants generally come directly from the energy industry, rather than from other search firms, because it is essential that everybody at the company be on the same page with respect to the recruiting knowledge. During the initial training period, recruiters accompany senior level management by attending meetings and interviews with our clients, to establish the credibility and rapport that our firm requires.

Successful Search Strategies

One of the key strategies that will help a company grow and become profitable is a focus on vertical specialization within the energy industry—specifically hiring high integrity professionals from within a specialized sector. By being a narrowly focused and distinct boutique search firm, the recruiting will be more successful in exactly what the clients are looking to receive as candidates.

Success is also based on the collaborative approach to recruiting. Each search is a team effort; typically two or three recruiters will meet with each client. Unlike many other search firms we do not have any researchers or account reps. When we go in as a recruiting team, we do the research; we do the candidate contact; we do the client presentation. It is a truly seamless process. This will avoid ambiguity and pinpoint the right candidate for all our clients.

At many generalist search firms, a researcher will gather up names of potential candidates from lists of executives who work at the client's competitor companies and make the initial contact. Many times these researches are not up to speed or as fluent as the consultant who has met with the client. We believe in doing our own research. Our firm's focus is so narrow that we already know and have met with most of the top candidates.

However, one of the biggest challenges that many search firms face these days involves overcoming compensation and equity package issues. Many executives in the energy industry are reluctant to leave their current employer if they are already well compensated; therefore, often it is necessary to find other ways of attracting a candidate, perhaps by pointing out that the client has a more aggressive business model and it is more in line with the risks that the candidate likes to take.

Assessing the Client's Business Model

Assessing a new client's business model and determining the type of candidates that will meet their needs is easier when you are a boutique search firm. Most of our clients are oil companies; we also serve a few energy service companies. As a result of our defined industry focus, we typically are able to already discern a great deal about how our client's business model works from the outset.

There are three main sectors of the oil and gas industry—the upstream, midstream (transportation and distribution of hydro-carbons), and downstream (refining and marketing)—and we specialize in the upstream, which involves exploration and extraction of oil and gas. Since we are extremely familiar with our client's specific industry focus, we are able to discuss other companies in the industry we have worked with, and as we develop a picture of the client's business model we will note how that model is similar or dissimilar to other companies in their sector, and how those common points or differences are likely to affect the client's search. When meeting with a new client, always try to determine their strengths and successes; tolerance to risk; and their need for complementary skill sets to shore up any weakness on their team.

Knowing the client's expectations is vital in the search. We educate them on what the search process entails, so that there will be no or few bumps on the road to a successful search. We always try to get the client to work in concert with us, so that we not only bring qualified executives to the table, but get them in the door and hired. Interviewing executives all day long is pointless if the process does not ultimately result in a fruitful hire.

Screening Candidates

Most often, I will begin the search process by talking to a number of leading people in the energy industry. I will describe the type of candidate that I am trying to find—i.e., what soft and hard skills our client needs. If a half dozen people come up with the same candidate name, then in most cases he or she could be the right candidate. In such cases, the candidate has been reference checked by the best in the industry—and then it is my job to engage the candidate's interest and bring him or her to the table.

After the initial interview, if there are any particular areas that my client has questions about, I will do some intensive reference checking. This process does not merely include the references that the candidate gives me. In most cases you know that such references will speak highly of the candidate; a candidate will not list references that he or she has had conflicts with in the past. Therefore, I will also discreetly have a discussion with the candidate's peers or former supervisors. One of the benefits working in a niche section is that I may know the people who worked with the candidate, and I can call them in order to discuss the candidate's good and bad points. I then provide my client with all of that information, and they will sift through it and make the final decision.

A Quality Focus: The Importance of Client Feedback

We are the world's oldest and largest retained search firm geared exclusively to the exploration and production sector of the energy industry. Quality is endemic within our firm, and integrity is paramount. Indeed, we turn down work due to time or capacity limitations, because we want every search to have our complete attention. As a result, we complete 97 percent of the searches that we are retained on, which is substantially above the industry average. Our company attracts new business thanks to word of mouth reports from satisfied clients. I believe that if you do your job well and keep the clients happy, they will keep coming back to you and they will promote your company within their industry—and that is the advantageous method of marketing.

After completing a search for a new or existing client, we sit down with the interested parties—i.e., the head of HR, COO, or CEO—and do a post-audit of the search process.

- Did we live up to the client's expectations?
- What did they perceive as lacking in the work that we did?
- Inform the client if you believe that the search could have gone better, based on their actions and behavior—i.e., did they conduct interviews in a timely fashion; make rapid decisions; understand the hard work that we put into the recruiting process?
- Discuss those areas where you believe that the client may have been deficient and where they excelled, and hopefully they will do the same with respect to evaluating our service.

Gaining Market Share

A search firm's ability to take market share away from its competitors is generally put to the test in what is called a "shoot-out," which is the term used to describe a situation where a company needs to hire an executive, and then calls three search firms that work in that industry to compete for the job. In some instances the potential client already knows which firm they want to go with, but interviews other firms to cover all areas. However, if it is an honest "shoot-out," we try to win the client's search by positioning ourselves with respect to our in-depth understanding of the industry—our twenty-eight years of experience in working in the worldwide oil and gas sector.

We let potential clients know that not only will we deliver the candidate what they want and need, we will also find candidates that may not meet all of the client's specifications or qualifications, but who are considered natural athletes—candidates who are likely thriving in the current position yet have more potential to contribute laterally or move upwards.

Go the extra mile for the client! Instead of running a 10K for your client, run a marathon search for the client. Indeed, I believe that it is the depth of our understanding of the marketplace and our clients' business models, as well as our longevity in the industry, which has enabled us to achieve success and gain market share.

Client Development Strategies

The primary aspect of a CEO that has a direct financial impact on the company is involvement and activity in client development. I share many outside activities with the officers of our client companies, which provides for good networking opportunities. In addition, I supervise quality control with respect to almost all of the searches that are done by our company. I assist in developing leads for bona fide candidates, and help to ensure that our searches meet our clients' needs. As a CEO, I take care to steer the search firm in the right direction and away from the shoals and rocks that many firms in this industry encounter. Based on my background and experience in this industry, it is a simple cause and effect measure; I believe that if you perform for your clients, your revenues will take care of themselves.

A measure of success can be found in terms of the achievements of the executives we have put on board at our client companies. We have found that many of the candidates that we have placed have excelled in their new positions. If we have done multiple searches for a company we will typically keep track of how many of our placed candidates have been promoted, and how many are now true leaders. Those statistics tell us just how successful we have been in terms of finding the right executives for our clients' positions.

Recent and Upcoming Trends

The executive recruiting industry has gained a great deal of acceptance over the past twenty years. Many companies in the energy industry have come to realize that a CEO of a successful search firm must be just as skilled as a CEO of a successful oil and gas firm—and this realization has resulted in more acceptance and reliance on executive search as a key management tool.

One of the upcoming trends for the executive search firm involves benchmarking activities. For example, a conflict of interest may arise when a client asks the firm to interview a VP of Production who is being considered for a COO position, while also paying the firm to recruit potential COOs from other companies. In such cases, it would be best if the client hire a consultancy company that deals in that area. If the firm specializes in outside recruiting it would not fit this search, whereas internal recruiting falls into the realm of building the behavioral brain trust. Some other CEOs of search firms may attempt to undertake both activities, but it is good for a search firm to specialize and focus in their area of expertise.

Overcoming Difficulties

One of the most difficult aspects of working in the executive recruiting industry takes place during the first five years of a new search firm's existence, when a company is working to establish credibility in the industry. It is very difficult for a recruiter at a new search firm to tell a potential client, "If you retain me you can count on me; I am the only source that you will need for this search." Indeed, it takes a while to build credibility in this industry, and the only way to succeed in that effort is through successful performance and by building long-term relationships with your clients.

Another difficult aspect of being an executive recruiter is maintaining the quality of your searches; maintaining a healthy balance of ego and empathy when dealing with candidates and clients; and never being too greedy in terms of taking on too much work. You have to strive to maintain your integrity and the quality of your work, because while it can take ten or twenty years to establish a good reputation in this industry, it may only take a couple of years to tear it down. Maintaining your integrity and performance within the industry is vital.

The Importance of Innovation

There is normally not a great deal of innovation in this industry, although there has been some innovation in the area of e-recruiting. Although we use the Internet to assist us in the search process, we believe that you need to have direct contact with your candidates. We have found that most of those who respond to Internet recruiting sites are typically unemployed, unhappy, and unqualified. It is difficult to deal with candidates that the firm does not know; I am fortunate in that I have direct access to many high performance individuals. These potential candidates know that there is not a lot of downside involved in taking the time to consider what I have to say about a potential job opportunity—and there could be a lot of upside.

Indeed, when the Internet was first developed, e-recruiting was touted as the new way to go in the search industry. A lot of companies have tried to rely on e-recruiting as a search strategy, but it may not actually be an effective means in most cases. You have to reach out and entice someone with your job offer if you want to succeed as a recruiter. Only a generalist employment agency can rely on e-recruiting. E-recruiting is an innovation that has not made its mark in retained executive search.

At our executive search firm, our success depends on making sure that all of our consultants and VPs maintain high quality standards of performance. At the present time, we feel that our company is the right size; therefore, we are not specifically looking to grow. In the years to come, our search firm, like others in this industry, may be able to expand our efforts laterally in other areas within our client companies—i.e., if a recruiter is presently searching for technical manufacturing executives, they can also start recruiting for financial executives of manufacturing companies, or other generalist areas.

Alex E. Preston has more than thirty years of operating company and energy executive search experience. Formerly associated with Conoco in operations engineering, he was responsible for engineering evaluations, field coordination, planning, contracts, and management development. Mr. Preston has conducted search activities ranging from executive management to staff positions worldwide.

He holds a Bachelor's degree in mechanical engineering from Michigan State University and is a member and former committee chairman for SPE and API.

A Focus on Client and Candidate Objectives: A Comprehensive Approach to Ensuring Success

Cynthia Chandler
Principal

Brad Chandler
Principal

Chandler Group Executive Search

Aligning Objectives

Our search firm has a dual focus: about 50 to 60 percent of our practice is in the health care sector, which is conducted on a national basis, while the remainder of our practice involves generalist searches with a regional concentration on behalf of financial services, manufacturing, nonprofit, and technology-related companies. We typically work at compensation levels starting at $100,000.

When we launched the firm in 2001 we brought some strong beliefs and practices to the table which align our process with the objectives of our client organizations and the career goals of the candidates with whom we work. Our primary focus continues to be on contributing to the success of our clients' businesses, as opposed to achieving a certain revenue number within our firm, or reaching a certain number of searches or placements each quarter. We both encountered search firm environments where the emphasis was on building revenue streams and profits, while far less time was typically spent on initiating thoughtful actions that would enhance our client organizations. We decided to take an approach to the search process that was totally focused externally on clients and candidates when we created our own firm. Indeed, the mission statement that can be found on our Web site states: "We are focused on your success" as opposed to focusing on our own success.

Of equal importance is that we extend that focus to the success of our candidates as well as our clients. In the late 1990s, the search process had become extremely transactional because search firms were very busy. It was not uncommon to find recruiters working on too many searches at any given time, clients' needs were intense and urgent in that robust market, and competition to fill searches was fierce. As a result, the professional growth objectives and personal needs of the candidates were often overlooked. However, at our firm, we feel it is critical to pay as much attention to the needs of the candidate and their family as we do to the success of the client's organization. They are, to our view, tightly interwoven.

Hybrid Revenue Model with a Guarantee

As a retained search firm, we work for clients at senior management levels; and these clients pay our fee in three installments while we are conducting their search. Consistent with the industry standard, our fees are normally 33 percent of the first year annual compensation. However, we utilize what may be considered a hybrid retained model, in that we leave the last one-third of our fee uncollected until a job offer has been made and accepted. At that point we will send out an invoice for the remaining portion of the original estimation of the fee based on targeted compensation adjusted to the actual compensation package offered to the candidate. We provide the level of quality work that is typically expected from a fully retained search firm, and offer a formal guarantee with respect to the placement of our candidates. If a placed candidate leaves voluntarily or is released by the client for performance related issues during the first twelve months of employment, we will conduct the search for a replacement candidate with no additional search fees billed to the client. We take significant measures to ensure that this does not happen as it is highly disruptive to our client organizations and places a negative mark on the newly hired candidate's career. This "guarantee" excludes candidates who leave for reasons other than job performance such as change in ownership, organizational realignment and/or restructuring that shifts the level of responsibility from the original and/or materially changes the job description that was portrayed to the candidate at the time of hire.

Build Lasting Partnerships with Clients

In order to operate an effective and efficient search practice, professional search consultants need to build deep, productive, and long-term relationships with their clients. Two key ways to accomplish this are: 1) Through the deployment of the latest search technology that enables access to information about highly talented individuals and an in-house technology platform to effectively warehouse and utilize data and 2) Offering best practices that create a highly service oriented approach to client organizations. We believe that shortcuts in those two key areas cannot be taken. It is clear that continuing revenues and increased profitability are generated by establishing a close partnership with our clients, and those true partnerships ensure repeat business. Our overarching goal is to achieve and maintain a "preferred partner" status with our client organizations accompanied by the expectation that when they need the services of an executive search firm, they will call us first. We believe that success will come to our firm only after we deliver highly successful search outcomes to our clients. We suggest that if we consistently deliver success, we will never need to worry about declining revenue streams at our firm. Indeed, any search firm's growth and long-term existence depends on maintaining a volume of repeat business; such business is especially profitable because it does not require spending a significant amount of time working on business development strategies and tactics. Therefore, a search firm's ability to consistently deliver a quality search outcome will help to build its reputation in the marketplace—and achieving such a reputation is the best way to produce and increase long-term revenues and margins.

Web-based resources are both numerous and expensive but must be employed by search firms in today's market to offer clients the services they are expecting and require. Today, even small boutique firms like ours can acquire access to and information about millions of executives, each one of whom may be the key to locating and recruiting the very top talent to our client organization. This broad and deep pool of information will ensure the client is getting what they paid for and set the stage for success and long-term relationships. Related to this access is the technology to retain key pieces of information on an in-house platform that will permit thorough and thoughtful data sorting processes to turn the data into meaningful information during the search process. Efficient and dependable processes for resume storage, digital key word identifiers, computer generated connections that exist between individuals in the database, attaching resumes and personal information to search files, key personal attributes, compensation, search status labels that remind the consultant of where the potential slate of candidates are in the process, calendar and content entries for each activity around candidate and client contacts, are just a very few of the tools needed to serve clients effectively in the search process. Long-term client relationships often depend on the ability to quickly create search reports that get information to the hiring managers about the current status of the assignment, timelines, snapshot executive summaries, and comparative data on the slate of candidates. Providing timely, accurate, and thorough information to clients is indeed a "best practice" that helps them feel they are getting high touch and valuable services from their search consultants. Those same clients will have little incentive to seek other search firms as their partners.

Valued-Added Search Process

In addition to superior technology married with a best practice approach to serving clients, we try to add value to every step of the search process for both our clients and our candidates—and that value-added emphasis begins before we launch the public aspects of the search and continues all the way through post-placement follow-up, which may be a year or more after we have placed a candidate in a client company. Our process is flexible enough to meet each client's and candidate's individual needs and preferences while, at the same time, never compromising on the quality of the process.

Moreover, we are always looking for ways to partner with our clients outside of the search process, whether that entails making introductions to other consultants; sharing best practices in a given industry or discipline; or sharing resumes that are unrelated to our current search, without a fee if this process leads to a successful hire. For example, we may be working on a COO search for a client, but if that company is also looking for a director of marketing and we know someone who we think will be good candidate for that position, we will send the client their resume, with the candidate's permission—and there is never a fee attached to that service because it is part of our focus on our client's success; we think of such an exchange as "friends helping friends."

Analyzing the Client's Business Model

We also believe that there must be total alignment at the early stages of the search and not only on the part of the client's hiring manager, but on the part of anyone who will be interacting with the new hire—with respect to the description of the position that is being offered, and the qualifications that the candidate needs to bring to that position. We will always work closely with the client in that process, and our overall strategy involves taking a highly consultative and organizational development approach to the search process.

Therefore, one of the first things that we do when taking on a new search is to conduct a very extensive site visit where we will talk not only to the client's hiring manager, but to all of those individuals that will interface with this particular position ranging from board members to direct and indirect reports, and vendors. We like to get input from a number of people that can help us to understand the key characteristics of this position, and how the client's corporate culture looks and feels. In some cases, we will talk to former employees, outside consultants, competitors, vendors, and customers in order to gain a complete understanding of how the client organization functions; how decisions get made; and what weak spots might exist.

Obtaining this information is critically important as we want our candidates to have a good handle on the position we are asking them to consider. This information also allows us to make a full assessment of the types of strengths that we are looking for in a candidate, and we always want to prevent a duplication of skills within a given department. For example, if we are doing a CFO search and we know that the client has a very strong controller, that knowledge allows us to focus on finding candidates who are strong in other areas, such as compliance, strategy, M&A, or regulatory issues.

We also utilize an online assessment tool, coordinated by an external certified consultant that helps us to ensure that there is a mutual understanding among all the constituents in the client organization with respect to what the job entails, the skills that are needed in order to do the job, and the style in which the job must be performed. This "benchmark" is a single report that is a compilation of a Benchmark Development Assessment taken electronically by each search consultant working on the assignment, and the key stakeholders in the client organization including those who will interview the candidates at the client site. Together we create a document that indicates what we each think we are seeking in terms of abilities, motivations and interests, and personality traits.

Any discrepancies are then addressed by our external consultant and discussed thoroughly until there is full agreement about what it is exactly we are all going to be looking for as we move to candidate selection.

Later in the process, our slate of final candidates will fill out online an assessment instrument seeking information about them on those same parameters of abilities, motivations and interests, and personality traits, and those are then graphically juxtaposed on the benchmark to help us determine the best fit. We advise our clients to use this tool for no more than 25 percent of their hiring decision process. Thorough interviews and detailed references are still weighted most heavily. This unique assessment process is a strong differentiator for our service, in that it typically results in a much better end product.

Frankly, we have found that a candidate is rarely asked to leave an organization because of lack of skills; in most cases it is the candidate's behavior, interpersonal skills, and cultural fit that lead to failure in the hiring process. That is why it is so important for a search firm to spend as much time on analyzing the client's culture as they do on analyzing the candidate's skills.

In some cases, we will also participate in the client's onsite interviews of our candidates. It is helpful for us during these interviews to observe the interactions between the candidates and those they may eventually work with at the client organization. In addition, we may serve as moderators for some of these discussions if they are not well orchestrated. Finally, it gives us yet another opportunity to hear what questions the clients are asking the candidates which, of course, is yet another revealing activity as to their key interests in what the position is going to require.

Information gained from all these interactions is invaluable as every time we conduct a search with our clients we learn more about their organization, which enables us to do a better job on the next assignment with them.

Challenges in Finding Candidates

There are always a number of challenges involved in finding the right candidates for our clients. Most importantly, we have to find people who have the right skill sets for the client's position, and those skills sets are generally highly defined, based on the client's needs at a particular time, although those needs are always subject to change.

Once we thoroughly assess the client's needs, we typically look for candidates who have "been there and done that" in a similar organization, and more importantly, have done it successfully. We then consider the fit issue. While we clearly need to make sure that the candidate has the specific skill sets that are needed to do the client's job, we also need to know whether the candidate will be able to work in the client's environment successfully. It is important to develop a good sense of where a particular candidate will fit best—we do not want to place a candidate in an environment that is not rewarding for them, and we do not want our client to hire with a candidate that cannot do their job successfully.

Making sure that there is alignment between what the client is looking for and what the candidate is seeking is always a huge challenge. That is why we spend so much energy in the assessment phase for both clients and candidates. In addition, our clients are only interested in interviewing the top 15 percent or so of candidates in any given field; therefore, another major challenge that we face is not just finding people that can do the client's job, but the top people that can do the job with the greatest successful impact.

Relocation is often another significant issue—i.e., the willingness of the candidate to relocate. We work in second and third tier cities as well as major cities, and for example, a top candidate may have a child who is presently in a good school district, and therefore, they will not want to move. We always try to be very sensitive to such situations, because we have found that relocation typically creates many challenges for candidates as well as many opportunities. Challenges include leaving family members, friends, community groups, favorite health care providers, homes that have been the locations for fond memories, the hassle factor of selling and moving household goods, and the risk involved with a new job and new people. Opportunities are often the flip side of those very things like meeting new friends, buying or building new and nicer homes, a change of scenery, and most certainly creating significant impact on a new organization.

A major challenge to a professional search consultant is finding talented executives who can do the job the client requires while at the same time advancing their own careers with greater responsibilities and opportunities to grow professionally.

Reference Checking Procedures

To ensure that we produce the best candidates for our clients, we conduct extremely thorough reference checking procedures. First, we have extensive conversations with the references that the candidate has given us. In this formal reference checking process we do not utilize a standard list of questions that remain the same for every candidate. Our reference tool is customized and focused on the particular candidate for that particular search. For example, if we have three candidates for a particular search, the reference questions that we ask will be different for each candidate because we may need to corroborate certain pieces of information, or we may have doubts about certain areas. In addition, the client may have certain key areas of interest, and in those instances we like to confirm that our candidates have those particular abilities and skill sets. Some of those requirements may show up during our online assessment process, and those results can vary from search to search. Therefore, we will always probe quite deeply into any areas that may have come out of that assessment. It is not uncommon for our reference checking process to last well over an hour, and we believe that is relatively rare in the search business.

Another important tool that we use in the reference checking process is our nationwide network of trusted contacts. We often find that one or more of those contacts have worked with the candidate in the past, or they may know someone who has done so. These contacts are what we call informal or deep references. Indeed, we often attempt to speak with individuals other than the references that the candidate has given us, although it is particularly important to note that we will not do so if such an interview could expose the candidate's interest in looking at our client's job to his current employer. Finally, we use a third party reference checking process to verify the candidate's education credentials, employment track, criminal history, and credit history.

Measuring Success

We believe that it is important to monitor the ongoing success of the companies and candidates that we bring together. We are always happy to hear from clients who remain satisfied years after hiring one of our candidates, especially if they tell us that the candidate has surpassed their expectations in terms of helping their company grow and implement significant changes. We are equally pleased to hear from candidates who tell us that they love their jobs, and who thank us for placing them in wonderful organizations. That is how we gauge the success of any search process. It's not the placement, but the long-term success for both parties that really matters most to us.

We have found that it is far more important to our clients for us to focus on the ability of our candidates to do the job rather than there ability to get the job. Many recruiters are primarily focused on helping the candidate get the job, as opposed to making sure that the candidate can actually do the job. Some agencies coach candidates with respect to making sure that they are wearing the right suit or that they "look the part" for the client's job. However, if we coach the candidate at all, our focus is always on making sure the candidate expresses clearly their abilities, skill sets, and motivations to do the job—and that is a huge difference. Indeed, we celebrate the success of the search process not at the time of placement, but one or two years later, when we find that the candidate is in a rewarding job, and has added value to the client organization. Achieving that dual level of success, however, requires a thorough understanding of what the client's job is all about, and it requires making a very thorough assessment of the candidate. It is far easier to get a candidate hired than it is to make sure that the candidate can actually do the job over the long haul. That is why we spend so much time being disciplined around these critical search processes being described.

The Follow-Up Process

Therefore, the search process never ends at the moment of hire. Our firm utilizes a formal on-boarding process which is done through an outside consultant over the first ninety days after a hire. If we find that the candidate is starting to get misaligned or is struggling with certain issues early on, or if the hiring manager reports any difficulties, then our outside consultant, who has a neutral interest with respect to all parties in the search process, will deal with that situation in order to mitigate any difficulties going forward.

Our on-boarding process is based on Harvard Business School's study of the critical first ninety days of employment. The model is from the book written by Professor Michael Watkins at Harvard entitled *The First 90 Days*. We use an external consultant to conduct three meetings during that time. The first is typically with our external consultant, the new hire, and the lead search consultant. The second meeting is with the external consultant, the new hire, and the hiring manager and the third is normally with the external consultant and the new hire only. The keys are to map personal strengths and weakness against what needs to be accomplished, ensure that the new hire is making the correct assessment of the role and its related challenges and opportunities, building productive working relationships and generating early successes that establish credibility and create momentum, and building teams and gathering the support necessary to be successful.

Indeed, we stay in touch with our clients and candidates long after the placement is complete. During that follow-up process, we often gain helpful insights that can help us to correct certain issues with respect to the new hire. For example, if the client originally told the candidate that their job would entail certain duties, and they change that job description after the fact, it stands to reason that the candidate may not be comfortable with their new job, or that they may not be able to perform certain tasks. If we stay in touch with both parties after the hire, we can normally head off potential problems before they escalate to become more serious issues.

Marketing Strategies

Our search firm does no formal marketing, because we believe that the only way to market your product in this industry is to demonstrate that you have been successful in the past—and if you are successful, word gets out. Accordingly, if we are speaking to a prospective client we will always refer to our track record and give them examples of some great success stories we have been involved with. For example, one of our major clients is a large health care organization. When we were first hired by that client, they were facing multiple challenges around leadership continuity, organizational structure, and financial stress. One of our principals was retained to conduct a series of key searches aimed at helping their company turn around and continue a rich tradition of leading-edge initiatives. Since that time we have completed nearly fifty searches with that client, and we have placed the majority of their management team—a team that went on to win a national award for being America's top health plan leadership team!

Another way that we market our company on an informal basis is by staying involved in the community. For example, we may volunteer our time to work with consulting and outplacement firms with respect to executive search strategies, we are always open to attending HR association functions, and we work with nonprofit groups and associations in order to assist these organizations to grow and improve and help their people have more rewarding careers. Often, these companies do not have funds budgeted to focus on these areas, and we are eager to assist to make our own community a more inviting place to live and work. These volunteer activities often put us in contact with like-minded leaders from the business community with whom we may build professional relationships down stream.

Incorporating Client and Market Feedback

When we began to create the vision for Chandler Group, we asked some of our friends, clients, and others in the industry one key question—What do you like, and what do you dislike about the search process? Indeed, whenever we make a sales presentation, we will ask the prospective client what they liked and disliked about working with search firms, and through the years we have taken many suggestions from our clients and incorporated them into the best practices that we use at our search firm. For example, we do not send through any extra administrative charges for things like office expenses, phone charges, making travel arrangements, etc., to our clients, as is common at many other firms.

In addition, whenever we go out on a sales presentation we make it very clear to the client who is going to be working on their search. When clients work with a large search firm, they often find that the person who sold the search is not the senior executive who will be working on their search, and that situation can be very frustrating. Indeed, many of our clients have told us that one of the most negative aspects of the search process is being sold a search by a well-educated, well-dressed senior executive search consultant, who then is rarely involved until it is time to present the candidates, leaving people in the search firm's back room to do the actual search. Therefore, although our search firm does utilize the services of support teams, those team members always stay in close touch with the client, attend meetings, talk with the client frequently, and work closely with the senior people in our firm who also do most of their own research.

We also believe that it is very important to listen to what our clients are saying throughout the search process—we will stop using a certain strategy if the client does not want us to use it, or we will implement new strategies if that is what the client wants and needs. In almost every discussion that we have with a new client we will ask them what has frustrated them in the past in terms of working with search firms. In our client materials we make it clear that while there are certain key things like a thorough site visit, alignment of the job requirements among all stakeholders, complete and detailed candidate interviews and references that cannot be compromised in order to ensure successful search outcomes, we are always ready to be flexible and conduct a search based on the client's specific needs.

Difficult and Least Understood Aspects of the Search Process

One of the most difficult aspects of working in this field is dealing with the fact that most people do not realize what an executive search process actually entails. An executive search does not simply involve finding jobs for your friends or other people that you know; it means doing a lot of hard research, data collection, and exploring in order to find the best candidates for your client's position. A good search consultant must always be highly curious and ready to explore many layers of knowledge in order to truly understand the complexity of an industry, or the hidden talent—or lack of talent—of a candidate. Indeed, many people are quite surprised when they learn the level of detail and the amount of pure hard work that is required in the average search process.

The visible part of the search is when we are out meeting clients and candidates—conducting interviews, doing presentations, and spending a lot of face-to-face time with various individuals. However, many people do not realize the level of isolation that exists when you are in your office with your telephone headset on, and you are up to your elbows in online or hard copy research. In some cases, you may be in your office for twelve hours straight doing research and phone work leaving voice mail messages, talking to potential candidates, conducting deep phone interviews with interested and qualified candidates and frequent phone and/or e-mail updates to clients.

The face-to-face and more visible aspects of this business comprise only a small percentage of how we spend our time.

Many people who are outside or new to this industry are also surprised at the high level of rejection that executive recruiters experience. We are typically pursuing very passive candidates; many of these individuals have not even thought about writing a resume, much less relocating their family to another city or state—and some searches require candidates to move to less desirable areas of the country. Therefore, recruiters have to be prepared for the high level of rejection that results when you make those proactive phone calls. Indeed, it is not uncommon for us to make 300 to 400 phone calls for a search that will ultimately result in only ten to fifteen candidates, and half of those who seem qualified may suddenly decide that they are no longer interested in the position, or we may ultimately decide that they are not qualified, for one reason or another. Therefore, there is a great deal of rejection in this business, both on our part and on the part of the candidates, and while most recruiters are people-oriented, friendly, and outgoing, it can still be very difficult to be rejected thirty times in a row, or to tell twenty people that they are not going to be selected for a job. Even the best "people person" may not be comfortable in such a role.

Another difficult aspect of running an executive search firm is finding a way to balance your time between business development and working on your clients' searches. One needs to be constantly sensitive to the balance of giving the clients the time they deserve and require in filling their searches and during the same day making sure the search firm flourishes but keeping the business development pipeline full at all times. This is daily struggle for most search consultants and most of us are never quite satisfied with the balance at the end of the day as the work is never really finished when we leave the office.

Many people are also surprised to learn that there is a very important code of ethics in this business in relation to blockage—i.e., you cannot recruit nor should you ever think about recruiting from a client. As recruiters, we have access to extensive information about client companies and the talented executives within. At the same time, they have paid us a fee which has the implication that we are there to support them and advance their organization in every way possible. Recruiting talent from them is, of course, antithetic to that effort. Most firms will not recruit from a client for at least one year and often longer after a search has been completed. In addition to the foremost issue of ethics, it would, in our view, simply be bad business to "bite the hand that feeds you!"

The Successful Recruiter

In order to succeed as a search consultant, we believe that you really have to care a great deal about the success of the clients and the candidates with whom you are working. Therefore, we primarily measure our success based on the feedback that we receive from our clients and candidates about how well they are being served. Simply put, we do not have the privilege of measuring our own success—our clients and candidates measure our success. In essence, we believe that a successful search firm is a firm with satisfied clients and fulfilled well-performing candidates.

Many search firms measure success by how much revenue they have produced during a given month or quarter. Large search firms are in business to make money and return shareholder value. Therefore, their recruiters' success is frequently measured by how much revenue he or she has produced on a monthly or quarterly basis. However, as a small boutique firm, we do not measure our success in terms of revenue production, but rather on doing great search work. While we do not keep a running scorecard on our team members' revenue production, we always know exactly how well our team members are doing with respect to their client searches and client satisfaction. We monitor our recruiters' performance on a daily basis with respect to how many candidates they have found; what phase of the search the candidates are in; and whether the client is happy with the candidates we are presenting.

Golden Rules of Search

The first and foremost rule of the executive search process is that you do not recruit from clients as discussed earlier when we referred to "blockage." The second golden rule pertains to the ethics of confidentiality in this field. As executive recruiters, we typically learn many things about our client organizations, and much of this information is intended for use only with respect to our own assessment processes. It is not to be made public.

Our candidates also have the right to a high level of confidentiality. For example, we had to walk away from a search because the prospective client wanted us to turn over, on a weekly basis, detailed information about our entire list of potential candidates, information about candidates who withdrew from the search and the reasons why, as well as candidates who were not interested in the position and why they were not. They also wanted to know who we rejected and why we made that decision. We declined to provide that information as we feel strongly that it was not relative to the search and was not fully consistent with a Code of Conduct and Confidentiality from the Association of Executive Search Consultants (AESC) and certainly not aligned with our own set of ethical boundaries. We let the client know that we would tell them everything that they wanted to know about candidates who were qualified and interested in their job, but we would not discuss the other individuals with whom we had contact or potential candidates who had not yet agreed to be considered formally. Indeed, we feel so strongly about the concept of confidentiality with respect to candidates that we have notified the AESC about our views on this issue, as we have found that far too many search firms are acquiescing to clients' demands in this area. We feel it is an erosion of ethical practices that could eventually affect the search industry and ultimately our clients negatively. Executives will simply decline to talk with us if they feel their names will be provided to the marketplace when they have no interest or been rejected on an assignment. This could result in great candidates being unwilling to enter into the recruitment process fearing risk of exposure at their current job.

Our third golden rule of executive recruiting involves the importance of maintaining a full disclosure philosophy with respect to both clients and candidates. Simply stated, we are willing to tell our clients a great deal about our candidates, but we are also willing to tell our candidates a great deal about our clients, because we believe that both parties need to make highly informed decisions. For example, if we neglect to tell our clients about a candidate's weaknesses, or if we "forget" to tell candidates about certain aspects of the client company that may not be very positive—i.e., the company is currently involved in a lawsuit—it is likely that such negative information will come to light at some later point in time, and could potentially pose major problems post hire. We want both parties to have access to that information up front so that they can include it in their decision-making process.

The Importance of Innovation

Innovation in the search process is something that we are very passionate about. However, the benchmark with respect to new tools and processes is whether they can add value to the search process itself, or add value to the client and/or the candidate. That is why we have incorporated the front-end benchmark assessment to our search process, as well as our back-end on-boarding process; we feel both processes have added value to our organization, as well as to our clients and candidates.

In terms of technological innovation, we believe that all good search firms can have access to essentially the same information, the same data, and the same online databases and networking tools—it is simply a matter of how diligent they are about using them. For example, our technology is as robust and innovative as that of many large international search firms, and we use our technology very well to create extensive lists of potential candidates from around the nation and globe. In the years to come, we believe that we will see more innovation in the areas of online networking and background research; and we will always focus on acquiring those tools, practices, and information that can add the most value for our clients and candidates. Our own sophisticated database allows us to store, manipulate, recover, and process this information quickly and with key relational characteristics to each client's needs. This information is mapped to skill sets, experiences, past employment, colleagues in common from current and past employment, awards, public and intra-organizational recognition for achievements, and a host of other key characteristics helpful to the search consultant. Successful firms innovate with new technologies or fall behind quickly.

Upcoming Trends

New and emerging careers in the environmental and green initiatives industries will provide new areas of growth for many search firms in the years to come; and as search professionals, it is our responsibility to stay on top of new developments with respect to these global issues and industries. In addition, health care has always been a very important part of our search practice, and the health care industry continues to change and be challenged from many directions. On the political front, executives will be faced with addressing new questions around things like the proposed single payor system, reduced reimbursements from Medicare and Medicaid, consumer directed health, stem cell research, and an ever changing environment of regulatory initiatives. Moreover, disease management tools for conditions like congestive heart failure, diabetes, obesity, pulmonary disease, and geriatrics that can positively affect major areas of our population require new leaders and new ideas being brought to the marketplace. Issues like these offer challenges as well as growth opportunities for search professionals who will need to understand the complexities, current trends, and solutions to contemporary problems and know how to assess a candidate's ability to operate successfully in an ever-changing world.

We are also seeing a higher level of acceptance of small boutique search firms on the part of large client organizations. Many companies have come to realize that small search firms such as ours can be very nimble with respect to the search process; we can easily adapt to the client's needs, and we are not encumbered by the high degree of blockage we described earlier in this chapter that prevents search firms from recruiting from their current clients. The big firms have hundreds of clients from which they cannot recruit and that, of course, places limitations on the pool of candidates they can bring to their clients. With that comes the requirement that the boutique firms have built the data platforms that will permit them to locate that same large field of talented executives enjoyed by the larger firms. Frequently, boutique firms are selected because clients feel that we can offer a higher level of intimacy to them and to candidates, while performing at the same level as the large, multi-national search firms. Clearly, the "Big Four" search firms do great work and will always hold a significant place in our industry, but there is a definite trend towards the use of boutique firms, and we are clearly benefiting from that trend.

A Privileged Business

Indeed, we consider executive search a privileged business in that we have the privilege of serving our clients in very important ways that can effectively shape how their organizations grow while at the same time we have the privilege of working with some of America's brightest and most successful people each and every day. What job is better than that?

Cynthia Chandler began her career of executive recruiting in 1995. Prior to starting Chandler Group, she was a vice president at a prominent, regional executive search firm and began her search career with a New York based international search firm. She has served clients in a wide variety of industries including manufacturing, financial services, consumer products, nonprofit and professional services. Searches completed include the functional areas of finance, human resources, senior management, sales and marketing, communications, plant management, and operations.

Ms. Chandler's total commitment to client service and her reputation for thoroughness and industry knowledge is endorsed by her many repeat clients.

Prior to her career in executive search, Ms. Chandler spent fifteen years with American Express Financial Advisors and Piper Jaffray. She received her B.A. from the University of Minnesota and has been an active community volunteer for many years, serving on various committees and boards. She is very active in the civic and nonprofit community having served on several different boards.

Brad Chandler has conducted senior level executive search assignments throughout the United States since 1991. Prior to forming Chandler Group with Cindy Chandler, he was the managing vice president of the Minneapolis office of a national executive search firm focused on the health care industry.

127

Mr. Chandler assists his clients with the recruitment and retention of executives in the health care and managed care industries. He has conducted senior level search assignments for health plans, integrated delivery systems, hospitals, clinics, pharmaceutical manufacturers, PBMs, medical device OEMs, informatics companies and TPAs.

Many of the nation's leading health care organizations have developed long-term partnerships with Mr. Chandler to continuously assess the most effective organizational structures and select carefully matched executives to meet current needs and ensure long-term success.

Mr. Chandler, who holds a Bachelor of Science degree from the University of Minnesota, has previous experience as the vice president of operations and then chief executive officer of a firm specializing in market research for health care and technology companies, as well as a division involved in physician search. Mr. Chandler's experience and knowledge of effective leadership methods and styles benefit his clients when helping them to assess their organizational requirements.

Dedication: *Dedicated to the many wonderful clients, candidates, and colleagues with whom we have had the pleasure of knowing during our careers in executive search.*

APPENDICES

APPENDIX A

LAUNCHPAD FOR NEW HIRE

Would you like to:

- Clearly identify the challenges of your new assignment?
- Clarify the expectations and get the support of your new boss?
- Strategize on how to leverage your strengths and manage your limitations?

LaunchPad is a three-step process facilitated by Chandler Group to provide transition coaching to newly placed managers and executives.

Objectives

LaunchPad consists of 3 one hour sessions with an Executive Coach, recruiter, hiring supervisor, and HR person to help the new hire analyze their strengths, assess the challenges of the new position, and develop an entrance strategy to maximize their performance during the first few months.

The Process

First Meeting - The recruiter from Chandler Group and the Executive Coach meet with the new hire to clarify the challenges of the position as well as the new hire's personal strengths and limitations.

Second Meeting – Soon after the first meeting the new hire and Executive Coach meet with the supervisor to clarify the success factors for the position and measurable objectives for the first 3 months and first year.

Final Meeting - The new hire and Executive Coach meet about two months into the new assignment to track the new hire's progress against the transition plan, progress on the 3 month objectives, and make adjustments to the plan.

Confidentiality

Because the new hire is the client for the LaunchPad process, all conversations are confidential. No information collected by the Executive Coach will be shared with the hiring company except by the new hire or with the new hire present.

Courtesy of Cynthia Chandler and Brad Chandler, Chandler Group Executive Search

APPENDIX B

CHANDLER GROUP ENGAGEMENT LETTER

Chandler Group Executive Search, Inc. accepts the assignment on an exclusive basis for the position of Position for Company. This letter will set forth the terms under which Chandler Group will provide executive search services.

Chandler Group agrees to:

a. Interview Client for the purpose of developing a detailed profile outlining the specifications and requirements of the position. All proprietary information gained in these meetings will be kept in strictest confidence.

b. Identify, recruit, and evaluate candidates whom Chandler Group believes will meet the specifications provided by Client. We will then present to you information regarding each candidate to be interviewed.

c. Conduct candidate interviews to determine the technical competence, general character traits and compatibility with Client's management team.

d. We will use all efforts in our background investigation to identify critical areas of performance and traits indicated in the position description based on our previously agreed upon standards. Our review will entail in-depth conversations with the candidate and with references provided by the candidate or those who are known to us to have relevant information concerning the candidate.

e. We will conduct complete referencing of top candidates. We will include meetings and conversations with prior and current superiors, subordinates, peers, clients and persons who have had professional relationships with the candidates.

f. We will assist you in the selection process and in the development and presentation of an offer.

g. Chandler Group guarantees that every placed candidate will remain with the client company for a period of twelve months from his/her start date. If a placed candidate leaves voluntarily, or is released by the client company for performance-related issues during the first twelve months of his/her employment, Chandler Group, if notified within 45 days that the replacement search should begin immediately, will conduct a new search to replace the candidate for no additional fee (charging only expenses as incurred). This will be valid only if each invoice is paid within the parameters as set forth below. This guarantee excludes candidates who leave for reasons other than job performance, such as a change in ownership, organizational realignment and/or restructuring that shifts the level of responsibility from the original and/or material changes to the job description that were portrayed to the candidate at the time of hire.

Client agrees to:

a. Appoint Chandler Group as the exclusive recruiter for the position and facilitate the process by:

   - Furnishing a job description or general outline of duties and responsibilities.
   - Providing Chandler Group with a complete and timely evaluation of candidates presented.
   - Being responsive to inquiries from Chandler Group and being reasonable in the accommodation of schedules to ensure a timely interview process.
   - Maintaining confidentiality and agreeing not to verify credentials on any candidate without first notifying Chandler Group or the candidate.

b. Pay Chandler Group a fee equal to 33% of anticipated initial annual compensation for the position, including estimated bonus, signing bonus, and other cash compensation. Our fees are invoiced in three installments. The first will be invoiced upon the execution of this agreement. The second will be invoiced 30 days later and the third will be invoiced only upon successful completion of the search, which is defined as the successful candidate's acceptance of the offer. Our final invoice will incorporate any adjustments based upon the base compensation and any estimated bonus listed in the offer letter for the position filled. In addition to the fee, Chandler Group will invoice Client for out-of-pocket expenses incurred during the search process for food, lodging, and transportation for Chandler Group associates or prospective candidates. Any single expense projected to be greater than $500 will be preauthorized by Client.

c. Should candidates submitted by Chandler Group be hired by Client for other positions within one year of the date the resumes were received, Client agrees to pay a discounted and mutually agreeable fee to Chandler Group.

Either party may discontinue this assignment by written notification. In this event, you will be billed for expenses incurred to the date of cancellation and for professional fees as follows: Our first billing is a minimum retainer and will be due. In the event of any subsequent cancellation, payment will be required for the pro-rated portion of the remaining professional fee based on the number of calendar days after the date you sign this agreement to the 60th day. If a cancellation occurs after sixty days, all professional fees will be due in full, with the exception of the final installment, which is due only if an offer is made and accepted. If the search is placed on hold for a period exceeding 60 days, the assignment will be considered complete and the third installment waived.

An invoice will be issued and work on this search will begin immediately upon receipt of this signed agreement.

CHANDLER GROUP   **AGREED TO & ACCEPTED BY:**

Cynthia Chandler
Date: _____   **Date:** _____

Courtesy of Cynthia Chandler and Brad Chandler, Chandler Group Executive Search

APPENDIX C

CHANDLER GROUP PROPOSAL

Chandler Group is a retained executive search firm with a singular focus on the success of our clients. By forming true partnerships, we provide client organizations with the commitment and expertise to identify, acquire and retain top talent that will ensure organizational success in today's challenging business environment.

We do this with unwavering integrity, respect for all individuals, and total dedication to our long-term professional relationships.

WHY CHANDLER GROUP?

- We recognize that seasoned and proven executives are (client name)'s most valuable asset, and Chandler Group has a proven track record of providing the link to those individuals who will become a highly effective leader in your organization.

- We have over seven decades of combined executive search experience and have successfully completed searches in many industries including financial services, manufacturing, distribution, technology, healthcare, retail, non-profit, education, public relations, professional services and real estate. In these industries, Chandler Group has experience in all functional areas.

- We understand that every organization is facing unique challenges and provide a customized search strategy for each assignment.

- We have developed an extensive network of highly-respected contacts and business leaders throughout the nation who provide Chandler Group access to talented individuals who may not be actively seeking new opportunities.

- We have established a strong reputation for our ability to understand and appreciate the importance of balancing the technical skills and "chemistry and fit" of a candidate with the needs and culture of your organization.

- We share your sense of urgency and can complete your project quickly by utilizing state of the art technology, timely communication, in-depth industry knowledge and research, and an effective screening process that will quickly identify quality candidates.

- We have the ability to actively recruit candidates from a vast number of companies across the nation without the burden of client restrictions faced by large national search firms.

- We do not charge our clients additional administrative fees.

Chandler Group guarantees our results!!!

(CLIENT NAME)

"HITTING THE TARGET"

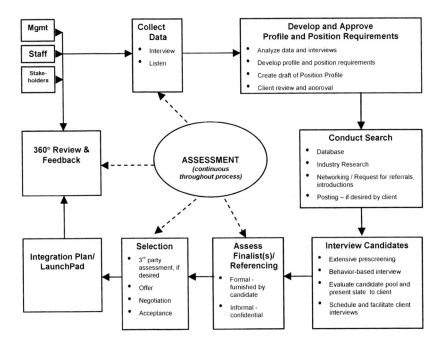

OUR SEARCH PROCESS

Chandler Group conducts each search assignment with the recognition that clients have unique needs and expectations. Within this custom-designed approach is a structured, comprehensive and proven process that ensures a successful and timely hiring decision.

At every phase of the process, it is our promise to represent (client name) in the best possible manner to all potential candidates and the market.

Phase One - Defining the Position and Developing the Search Strategy

1. Chandler Group will schedule and engage in detailed discussions with your key representatives to understand (client name)'s mission, values, culture, short- and long-term strategic objectives and your expectations relating to the position and the search process.

2. Chandler Group will gain a thorough understanding of your organization and will facilitate consensus on the position's responsibilities, reporting relationships, compensation, desired traits and required experience to successfully perform the job. In this process, we are prepared to offer our expertise and industry knowledge to help you create an opportunity that will be enticing to prospective candidates and will provide you assurance that this is a role that will most effectively contribute to your business goals.

3. A detailed Position Profile will be prepared and submitted for your approval. This document thoroughly outlines the key components of the job, an overview of (client name) and will serve as the basis for preliminary discussions with all prospective candidates.

4. A search strategy will be designed that incorporates a competitive overview, current industry conditions, research on target companies and candidates, identification of industry

leaders, review of our proprietary database, and our referral sources and established networks. This comprehensive strategy will quickly lead us to qualified candidates.

Phase Two - Identifying and Selecting Candidates

1. Chandler Group will identify and contact potential candidates, industry leaders, and our trusted network of professional sources. During these discussions, we discuss the specifics of the position, the culture of the organization, the background requirements and determine if there is interest in the position and whether or not there is a "fit" with (client name). If there are "internal" candidates that you want to consider, we will meet with them and incorporate them into our process.

2. From the continuously growing list of initially screened candidates, we conduct extensive interviews to review their qualifications, previous successes, areas of growth, and their motivation for their interest in your position.

3. As appropriate, we will begin the process of checking references on the candidates that will be presented to you for your review. We will discuss confidentially with others who know the candidates' technical skills as well as their leadership style and abilities.

Phase Three - (client name) Interviews, Evaluation and Selection

1. Candidate profiles and evaluations will be prepared and presented to you for review along with our recommendation for initial interviews by (client name).

2. Chandler Group then arranges interviews between you and the top candidates. Prior to these meetings, we will spend significant time preparing you and the candidates to maximize your time together. At your request, we can provide interview skills coaching to any of your team members. This important exchange of information between the two parties is one of the

most critical aspects of the search process. Subsequent meetings with the top "select" candidate(s) are recommended.

3.   As your top candidates are identified and selected, we will continue to conduct in-depth references to confirm the findings and impressions that have been developed during the previous steps.

4.   If you desire, we will arrange for professional assessment of your top candidates. This assessment is often valuable in validating your conclusions and can be used as the foundation for any career development plans that you have for the individual.

Phase Four – Offer, Acceptance and Follow Up

1.   Based on our candid conversations and our knowledge of the market, Chandler Group will assist you in the formation of an offer and serve as an intermediary in the negotiations. The interests of both (client name) and the candidate must be addressed to achieve the goal of an accepted offer. We will continue to counsel both parties around any outstanding issues, counteroffers, and career planning for the candidate.

2.   Upon acceptance of an offer by your selected candidate, we will begin the process of integrating and "on-boarding" your new hire. This is accomplished in a very disciplined process with a highly experienced executive coach. It will involve an initial meeting with the candidate and Chandler Group. The next meeting will be with the hiring manager and the follow up meeting will be with the new employee. These meetings will focus on coaching the new employee how to acclimate successfully within the first 90 days.

3.   We will remain involved with you and the successful candidate after the offer is accepted and the individual begins the process of transitioning into your organization. Our commitment to (client name) and your new employee continues throughout the following year to ensure that the objectives of your search are met.

LaunchPad for Integration of New Hire

LaunchPad, the last step of our rigorous search process, is provided by Chandler Group and serves to assist the new hire as they transition into their new environment.

Objectives

LaunchPad consists of 3 one-hour sessions with an Executive Coach, recruiter, hiring supervisor, and HR person to help the candidate analyze their strengths, assess the challenges of the new position, and develop an entrance strategy to maximize their performance during the first few months.

The Process

The process begins during Phase 1 of the search as Chandler Group analyzes the position and the challenges that will face a new candidate.

The process continues during Phases 2 and 3 of the search as Chandler Group assesses the strengths and limitations of potential candidates.

In Phase 4 of the search the recruiter from Chandler Group and the Executive Coach meet with the candidate who has accepted the position to discuss the candidate's strengths and potential challenges to help them develop a transition plan for the first 3 months.

During the first weeks in the new position the candidate and Executive Coach meet with the supervisor to clarify the success factors for the position and measurable objectives for the first 3 months and first year.

Finally, the candidate and Executive Coach meet about two months into the new assignment to track the candidate's progress against the transition plan, progress on the 3-month objectives, and make adjustments to the plan.

OUR FEES

Our fees are 33% percent of the first year's cash compensation. Our estimated fee is billed in three installments: the first one-third is due at the commencement of the search; one-third is due thirty days later; and the final one-third is billed upon successful conclusion of the search.

We are reimbursed only for travel expenses that are directly related to the search. We do not bill for additional expenses such as mailing expenses, cell phone and long-distance telephone expenses. We make every attempt to keep these expenses to a minimum and will not incur significant costs without your prior authorization. There are no additional administrative fees billed to clients.

Chandler Group offers a performance guarantee. Should the successful candidate leave during the first year of employment, we will find a replacement at no additional fee. You would pay only for the out-of-pocket expenses incurred on the new search.

REPRESENTATIVE CLIENTS

MANUFACTURING

- *Agriliance*
- *BMC Industries/Vision Ease*
- *Cargill*
- *CIMA Labs*
- *CNS*
- *Conwed Plastics*
- *Ecolab*
- *G & K Services*
- *Jostens*
- *Liberty Diversified Industries*
- *Minnesota Diversified Industries*
- *Nilfisk – Advance*
- *Park Industries*
- *TissueLink*

HEALTHCARE

- *Allina Hospitals & Clinics*
- *Blue Cross & Blue Shield of Iowa*
- *Cancer Treatment Centers of America*
- *Center for Diagnostic Imaging*
- *DakotaCare*
- *CBCA, Inc.*
- *HealthEast Care System*
- *Kaiser Permanente*
- *Medica Health Plans*
- *Minnesota Hospital Association*
- *Partners National Health Plans of North Carolina*
- *Stratis Health*
- *Summa Health System*
- *American Republic Insurance*
- *Assurant Health*
- *CBSA*
- *Ceridian, Lifeworks*
- *Hazelden*
- *HealthEquity*
- *Primary Health*
- *RedBrick Health*
- *South Country Health Alliance*
- *St. Mary's Duluth Clinic*

FINANCIAL SERVICES/ INSURANCE/BANKING

- *Fair Isaac*
- *Fortis Financial / The Hartford*
- *GMAC / RFC*
- *U.S. Federal Credit Union*

PROFESSIONAL & BUSINESS SERVICES

- *APM/Minnesota Public Radio*
- *e-Travel Experts / ACS*
- Hubbard Broadcasting
- *Right Management*
- *Ryan Companies*
- *Young America Corporation*

NON-PROFIT & EDUCATION

- *Animal Humane Society*
- *Big Brothers Big Sisters of Greater Twin Cities*
- *Children's Cancer Research Fund*
- *Corporation for Supportive Housing*

- *MacPhail Center for the Arts*
- *Mennonite Mutual Aid*
- *Metropolitan Airports Commission*
- *Minneapolis Aquatennial*
- *Minnesota Diversified Industries*
- *North American Bison Cooperative*

EXAMPLE SEARCH ASSIGNMENTS

SENIOR LEADERSHIP

- *Chief Executive Officer*
- *Chief Financial Officer*
- *Chief Information Officer*
- *Chief Intellectual Property Counsel*
- *Chief Marketing Officer*
- *Chief Medical Officer*
- *Chief Operating Officer*
- *Executive Director (Non-Profit)*
- *General Counsel*
- *Medical Director*
- *President*

MARKETING

- *Director / Sr. Director, Marketing*
- *Director, Business Development*
- *Director, Communications*
- *Director, Government Sales*
- *Director, Market Research & Intelligence*
- *Director, Product Management*
- *Director, Segment Marketing*
- *Segment Marketing*

FINANCE

- *Chief Financial Officer*
- *Controller*
- *Director, Planning*
- *Director, Planning & Analysis*
- *Plant Controller*
- *Vice President, Chief Actuary*

HEALTHCARE

- *(All Sr. Leadership Positions)*
- *Administrator – Nursing Practice and Education*
- *Administrator – Nursing Resource Management*
- *Associate Director, Supply Chain & Logistics*
- *Chief Medical Officer*
- *Medical Director*
- *Sr. Vice President, Managed Care*
- *System Director, Revenue Cycle Management*
- *Vice President, Medical*

Manager
- *Sr. Vice President, Business Segments*
- *Vice President, Communications*
- *Vice President, Marketing*
- *Vice President, Account Services*

Management
- *Sales, Sales Management*

HUMAN RESOURCES

- *Director, Compensation & Benefits*
- *Director, Human Resources*
- *Director, Organization Effectiveness*
- *Manager, Compensation*
- *Vice President, Human Resources*
- *Vice President, Labor Relations*
- *Vice President, Organizational Development*

OPERATIONS

- *Chief Operating Officer*
- *Client Services Manager*
- *Director of Operations (Call Center)*
- *Director, Project Management Office*
- *Plant Manager*
- *Vice President, Manufacturing*
- *Vice President, Technology & Supply Chain*

EXAMPLE SEARCH ASSIGNMENTS

SALES
- *Director, Business Development*
- *Division Sales Managers*
- *Major Accounts Manager*
- *Regional Director*
- *Strategic Account Manager*
- *Vice President, Key Account Management*
- *Vice President, Key Account Sales*
- *Vice President, Sales & Marketing*

NON-PROFIT
- *Director, Development*
- *Director, Major Gifts/Planned Giving*
- *Executive Director*
- *President*
- *Vice President, Information Services*

CONSULTING SERVICES
- *Managing Consultant*
- *Vice President, Consulting*

TECHNOLOGY
- *Chief Security Officer*
- *Chief Information Officer*
- *Chief Technology Officer*
- *Vice President-Information Systems*
- *Chief Architect*
- *VP Information Systems*
- *Director, PMO*

Courtesy of Cynthia Chandler and Brad Chandler, Chandler Group Executive Search

APPENDIX D

LAUNCHPAD FOR CLIENTS

LaunchPad, the last step of our rigorous search process, is provided by Chandler Group and serves to assist the new hire as they transition into their new environment.

Objectives

LaunchPad consists of 3 one-hour sessions with an Executive Coach, recruiter, hiring supervisor, and HR person to help the candidate analyze their strengths, assess the challenges of the new position, and develop an entrance strategy to maximize their performance during the first few months.

The Process

The process begins during Phase 1 of the search as Chandler Group analyzes the position and the challenges that will face a new candidate.

The process continues during Phases 2 and 3 of the search as Chandler Group assesses the strengths and limitations of potential candidates.

In Phase 4 of the search the recruiter from Chandler Group and the Executive Coach meet with the candidate who has accepted the position to discuss the candidate's strengths and potential challenges to help them develop a transition plan for the first 3 months.

During the first weeks in the new position the candidate and Executive Coach meet with the supervisor to clarify the success factors for the position and measurable objectives for the first 3 months and first year.

Finally, the candidate and Executive Coach meet about two months into the new assignment to track the candidate's progress against the transition plan, progress on the 3-month objectives, and make adjustments to the plan.

Courtesy of Cynthia Chandler and Brad Chandler, Chandler Group Executive Search

APPENDIX E

LAUNCHPAD PROCESS

Purpose

- Clearly identify the challenges of new assignment
- Clarify the expectations and get the support of new boss
- Strategize on how to leverage strengths and manage limitations

LaunchPad is program by the Chandler Group to provide transition coaching to newly placed managers and executives.

Objectives

LaunchPad consists of 3 one hour sessions with an Executive Coach, recruiter, hiring supervisor, and HR person to help the candidate analyze their strengths, assess the challenges of the new position, and develop an entrance strategy to maximize their performance during the first few months.

The Process

1st Meeting - The recruiter from the Chandler Group and the Executive Coach meet with the candidate to clarify the challenges of the position as well as the candidate's personal strengths and limitations.

- We call Barb to let her know that someone needs to be scheduled for LaunchPad. (generally need to leave voicemail, keep it short, "Barb – get your calendar and call")
- Barb calls us and we then conference call the LaunchPad participant (or admin) to schedule first session.
- At the end of the 1st meeting, Barb reviews next meeting schedule expectations: Participant (or admin) is to call Barb to schedule.

2nd Meeting – Soon after the 1st meeting, the candidate and Executive Coach meet with the supervisor to clarify the success factors for the position and measurable objectives for the first 3 months and first year.

149

- One week after the first meeting, we call participant (or admin) to confirm 2nd meeting has been scheduled. We can then note in database.

- At the end of 2nd meeting, Barb reviews next meeting schedule expectations: Participant (or admin) is to call Barb to schedule.

Final Meeting - The candidate and Executive Coach meet about two months into the new assignment to track the candidate's progress against the transition plan, progress on the 3 month objectives, and make adjustments to the plan.

- The 60-day Placement Genie will remind us to contact participant (or admin) to confirm final meeting has been scheduled. We can then note in database as COMPLETED.

Courtesy of Cynthia Chandler and Brad Chandler, Chandler Group Executive Search